TIMEI MAGICK –
The Basic Book of Spells

By Mitch Garlington

Contents

MAGICK INSPIRATION... 4

THE HEART OF A WITCH 5

RAINBOW WITCH 8

CHILDHOOD - PAST LIFE MAGICK 11

NATURE'S MAGICK 18
- TREES YOU MAY ENCOUNTER AND THEIR MAGICAL PROPERTIES 20
- THE ELEMENTS 22

BASIC WITCH'S ALTAR 25
- THE TOOLS 25
- DAYS TO PERFORM MAGICK - 28

MOON MAGICK 31

PROTECTION MAGICK 38

PSYCHIC ATTACKS 41
- HEXES 43

BANISHMENT AND BINDING MAGICK 53

ABUNDANCE AND PROSPERITY MAGICK 62

KNOT MAGICK 67

SELF HEALING MAGICK 71

DREAD WITCH 79

FORGETFUL MAGICK 83

BLESSINGS MAGICK 87

LOVE MAGICK 93

FERTILITY MAGICK 100
FRUITFUL MAGICK 106
    Vegetable Magick 114
CANDLE MAGICK 121
    Coloured Candle Meanings 121
CRYSTAL MAGICK 128
BASIC MAGICK 143
INDEX OF SPELLS 144
FRIENDS OF THE WITCH 147
GOODBYE BLESSINGS... 150

MAGICK INSPIRATION...

Once in a Purple Moon, there is a special young Witch who shines above the rest. Often they go unnoticed, because they are always out of step...

I have seen this witch trying to fly. I've watched them play, and seen how their friends have treated them!

A true Witch isn't always one who comes out on top of all the tests.

A TRUE WITCH has Witchcraft in them at all times... This is what you have... You're not the Worst Witch anymore...

(Grand Wizard - Jill Murphy)

THE HEART OF A WITCH

Brightest blessings and welcome... I am Mitch Garlington - Spiritual Medium, Psychic, Tarot Reader, Violet Flame Reiki Healer and Male Witch... Thank you so much for feeling drawn to purchasing my spell book.

From as far back as I can remember magick has run through my veins. People have often questioned my beliefs, and my ideas on how I see the world. People have said to me... *"are you sure you are not a warlock? or wizard? how can you be a witch you are not female?"* Where there is magick, sadly there is also ignorance.

No... I am simply a Male Witch.

Lesson one in Witchcraft - Always trust and follow your heart. Don't ever allow someone to project their-own fear or limitations on-to you. Being a Witch is not just about spells. It's a personal, ongoing journey of self-healing, self-acceptance, and self-discovery. Allowing yourself the freedom to beat to the rhythm of your own drum.

Growing up as a Witch has been an interesting time. Often, I have felt like a stranger in this world, an outsider, often on the edge of a circle looking in. But through all of the darkness magick has kept me alive and always played a part in my world in some shape or form.

I am what's known as an eclectic solitary Witch. This means I don't follow a set structure or pathway, I take pieces and inspirations from all forms of Witchcraft and blend them into my own personal way of working. I am for the most part a solitary Witch, this means I work solo and privately with my magick. I am blessed however, to have a few local witchy friends that gather on occasion to do rituals and spell work as and when we feel drawn to do so.

Why have I felt drawn to creating this book? I wanted to share with you a book of personal favourite spells and experiences, and to show how REAL magick can work and that it need not be stressful or complicated. How many times have you felt drawn to do a spell? Spend time finding one that's suitable but then discover... you need a never-ending array of herbs and ingredients etc. that you just don't have to hand. I mean, not everyone has a chicken foot or rabbits tail handy! (Don't get me wrong those spells have their place and can be powerful. But equally - so can basic Magick).

For me like with a lot of forms of energy work, people have a habit of over talking something and making it more complicated than it needs to be.

One thing I have learnt from being a Witch is magick is as easy or as difficult as you wish for it to be. It's a personal journey so ultimately you will find your own way of working. You will discover what does and doesn't sit right within your own sacred heart. - And this is the true power of a Witch.

The more powerful and original a mind, the more it will incline towards the religion of solitude - Aldous Huxley

RAINBOW WITCH

One question that I get asked a lot which always makes me chuckle, is how do I use my magick? Am I a good witch or a bad witch? or am I a grey witch?

I am neither light nor dark, black or white... I am a rainbow witch - I work with all the colours of the rainbow and use my magick accordingly. Because I am also a spiritual medium and healer I work with many different colours and forms of energy daily.

Magick for me is all about intention... Intention is KEY to making a spell work.

Words are a powerful thing. How many times have you had a bad day and wished someone bad luck in the heat of the moment. Then found out - that the person ended up having a run of bad luck on that very day. Words are like spell casting be mindful of what you are choosing to say, and how you say it.

Through both my witchcraft and my spiritual work, I am a big believer in karma and the power of three. What we send out we receive back threefold. Karma is something we cannot control or escape from. Quite simply, karma is like a rubber band, you can only stretch it so far before it comes back and smacks you in the face. Always try and send love out to the world and don't allow lower energy to rule your heart. (Easier said than done sometimes).

Therefore, with this in mind I try to use my magick for the highest of good. I would never abuse or misuse my magick to cause harm to another. If I did the chances are I would incur a karma debt which could come at a cost to me.

Whilst I will not misuse my gifts, in equal measure I will protect myself and use my magick to send unwanted energy or intentions back to source. This means that if another decides to misuse magick and project hurt or negative energy or a hex on-to me I will redirect it back to the sender. There is no excuse to send negative or hurtful energy to another just because you feel you can. This is wrong and in my own personal opinion a misuse of magick.

As with anything in this world there is good and bad, light and dark. We all have within us a shadow side. But it's about allowing the light in when working with magick. I also always look at a situation before I cast a spell... this means - do I think magick is the answer and will it benefit the situation for the highest of good? Sometimes it will, but not always. If it doesn't I won't do it... Simple...

Magick is not a quick fix so must be done with respect and the right intention. Intention is so important as it's the very thing that will allow a spell to work. How often have you said in your thoughts *"I really need something to go my way today?"*, you have said it with such a strong passion and intention. In return it has probably unfolded in a positive outcome for you. I know from personal experience that has always been the way for me.

Magic is the bloodstream of the universe. Forget all you know, or think you know. All that you require is your intuition - High Aldwin, Willow

CHILDHOOD - PAST LIFE MAGICK

People often ask me was I born a witch? How or when did I know? As I said at the beginning I have always felt magick within me, and I was indeed born a witch. This is interesting for me as nobody else in my family that I know of is. Some people come from a long-established family of witches and it runs down through their lineage. This is not the case for me, as far as I'm aware and from what I have researched I come from a family of muggles. (Non-magical or non-spiritually awoken souls if you are not familiar with the term).

I feel my witch energy is an old wise, ancient power, that actually stems way back in time from many past lives, a time when witches and wizards walked the earth, and the followings of the old ways were alive and very much a way of life.

Growing up was a tricky time for me... I was always different and felt like I was juggling a lot of balls in the air. I also felt I was constantly having to justify and defend myself from family members, teachers, and the everyday world. The great thing about when you're young is often you actually know exactly who you are and what you're about. For me, it was when I was at school and college that I was trying not to be conditioned to be a certain way! But this witch is stubborn... and I knew myself better than anyone.

I am a creative, I was also understanding my own magical gifts, as well as my spiritual gifts as spirit would often be around me, and I was exploring and understanding myself on a deeper level through sexuality. If I'm being honest with myself I knew I was gay from probably around the age of 4 or 5. People don't like it when I say this as they view you as a child, *"how can you possibly know anything at that age?"*. They basically choose to not want to hear it! I'm not sure why, is it a fear thing? As a parent do they question that on some level they've failed? I have amazing parents who have always guided me in the best way. I guess possibly parents have ideas and expectations on how they want their kids to be, but as long as they are healthy, happy, loved, and cared for, a parent's job is done. Allow that child the freedom to be them self and not project limitations on what you feel would be best. Growing up with my Dad was tricky at times! He is the head muggle in our family... He has a heart of pure gold and we do love each other dearly, but we see the world from completely different ends of the spectrum.

When you're a child of the earth there is no expectation from you, no demands from the physical world have been embedded or placed upon you yet. We choose to conform to those ideas later on, or not as the case maybe. So surely as a child even more so, you are aligned with self and know yourself more than ever before...

I've always had a weird energy around men and masculine energy in general. This started at school with male teachers and right through my work life until much later where I was able to break the cycle. These men hadn't done anything wrong really, it was just more their attitudes towards me. I seemed to be surrounded by low level masculine energy and attracting ignorant people who saw themselves as something special. They seemed to write me off or have a low tolerance for my ways because I was different.

At school, I would always gravitate and learn more from the female teachers, friends would mainly be female, later on it was the same with co-workers... especially in some of the larger business I have worked for. The men were a pain in the arse driven by ego, material wellbeing and greed! Everything I'm not interested in... so I kept my circles small with the female energy around me. I am very in touch and comfortable with my feminine energy, I think this is partly to do with my sexuality, but also linked to past life. I honour this part of me, for this is the Goddess energy that resides within me.

Part of my self-healing journey has been to understand, make sense and release these negative old patterns. Years later I was able to get my answers, it was like completing a jigsaw puzzle and suddenly all the pieces seemingly fitting into place, and I was made aware of a much bigger picture.

The first experience I had came in the form of a beautiful earth angel and friend called Beth James. Not only is she an amazing pure soul with one of the most beautiful hearts I know, she is also an amazing healer, reader, and astrologer...

I had an astrology reading with Beth to make sense and understand, what was happening within my birth and star chart. It's one of the best, if not, THE best reading I have ever had. Every question or thought I had was covered through the reading. It was like suddenly my life made complete sense as to why certain cycles and patterns had happened or were happening.

She covered everything on the masculine energy, which interlinked with my dad. She explained I had a large area that was for me being a teacher or mentor for others. My one regret is I wished I had recorded the reading. Just talking about it now gives me goose bumps.

Beth also explored a very important area that interlinked the witch within. I have a large area of Crone energy with my chart. This is why I've always felt older than I am, and comfortable with the female energy that runs through me. But also, why I am comfortable around more mature ladies or why they feel drawn to me. It went really deep and I can't remember all of it right now without really thinking back again. But the message I got through the reading was that I was always born a witch, the evidence is there literally within the star chart.

I have known various astrologers and never felt guided to have a reading with them. I know Beth just feels she is doing her job, but she gave me one of the most beautiful gifts I could have and for that I am eternally grateful.

The second experience was on more of a personal level and actually happened a few weeks after my reading with Beth. I was in the shower and was just chatting to myself as you do. I often go into little day dream or brief trance states. On this occasion I went much deeper and actually connected with a past life. I have never done past life regression through a practitioner before or anything like that, although I have been shown snippets before in meditation.

I went so deep with this energy it was like I was watching a movie in full colour. I was a head female witch in a previous lifetime, and I had a coven of all female witches, around 20 to 30 were being shown. I could see I was slender and tall with a beautiful body, pale skin and raven black long hair. I could also feel there was extreme pain and sadness within this witch's heart. As I continued to watch it was clear that she had a partner whom she loved but he betrayed her and broke her heart. She ended up poisoning him, and promised herself she would love herself, more than any man would again.

As I continued to watch she ran a coven that invoked magic both dark and light. This was to empower women and give them direction and purpose again. The more I watched the clearer it was becoming, how much she hated and despised men and all they stood for.

Suddenly once I was shown all they wanted me to see I was back under the hot running water of the shower. It felt like I had been gone for hours but in reality was probably, between 15 to 20 minutes. I straight away knew that I had experienced a past life energy. It's like whilst I was viewing I could feel every pain, every thought and feeling that this lady had gone through. In the end she was hung for being a witch and invoking the dark arts.

Suddenly more of the picture started making sense - I knew on a deeper level that some of what I am going through or have been through in this life-time is a karma debt from that previous time.

The pain she inflicted on men made sense to why I felt judged and uncomfortable around masculine energy. The fact I am gay and have felt at times I have not belonged. It's like the polar opposite of what this lady went through. She chose to use her magick through the dark arts as well as for good. Whilst I choose to practice my magick in light and love. It's like we are the yin and yang energy both connected and learning through each other.

It's also interesting when I do spirit work - Mediumship - one of the ways my guides make themselves known to me, is by a tightness around my throat. Almost like a rope being placed around my neck. This usually causes me to gag or cough, but then I am good to go. Whilst it's not a pleasant feeling, I know once I have that my guides are ready to work, and spirit magick can begin.

So, back to the original question, *was I born a witch?* You can see it's taken years for me to fully understand myself. But through these combined experiences you can see, that, yes it stems back from a very long lineage of its own, and I was indeed born a witch.

To remember who you are, you need to forget who they told you to be - Elphaba Wicked

NATURE'S MAGICK

People often ask me where is the best place to perform magick? it really does depend as magick is such a personal journey. Depending on what the spell is for can help with the location you use.

What I have found is whenever I perform a spell or incantation within nature, I tend to receive the best results. Nature for me seems to be the altar for any type of magical workings.

Nature shows itself in many beautiful and unique ways. To me its Mother Earth's temples... a place of complete stillness and connection with the ancestors and ancient spirits.

Be still and listen... the earth is singing...

By working within nature you have so many options available. It could be you have a beautiful garden in which you are able to perform magick a little easier. If this is the case it might be nice to set up an altar area. This then becomes a designated place you choose for doing spell work. The altar might sound grand but can be as basic or complex as you wish. I have a friend that has the tiniest garden and their altar is all inside a flower pot. I have another friend that lives in a flat and they have a small altar on the edge of a balcony section outside the window. There is no right or wrong way here, only your way.

The beauty of doing magick in a garden is you can also plant or may already have so many free ingredients on your doorstep. When the trees shed leaves, nuts, seeds - and berries - these can be used in spells, or when a flower releases a petal these can be dried out and used in spell work. A pink rose for a love spell for instance. The list is never-ending.

A magical tip - keep purple flowers by a window that faces the moonlight, to draw in healing energies to the third eye - and help open the window to the subconscious mind.

Some people do not have a suitable garden, may be overlooked or have problems with nosey neighbours (we have a spell for that! ... *evil cackle*...). If you fall into this bracket do not panic, there are many other options to choose from.

It could be you know of a beautiful wood or forest area nearby, that is quiet and the perfect location to find the stillness required to perform magick. After all the trees and the earth give away so much to us for free and ask for very little in return. Trees are the lungs of our planet - they clean the very air that we breathe, and we exhale what they need. Trees and people need each other. Have you ever gone into the woods and gone up and touched or wrapped your arms around a beautiful ancient tree? - If you haven't you must try this... you will instantly feel a wave of upliftment, unconditional love, strength, and healing. Trees and nature have the power to heal our mind, body and spirit.

Should you choose to work in a setting like this. Always ask in thought or aloud if it's ok to be here. Be mindful that these types of place do not only harness this realm, but they also allow the animal kingdom to take shelter, and other worlds such as fae and elementary energy to reside. Remember when we work with magick we work with the seen and unseen worlds, and we may call upon creatures from another time, place or dimension. (Be careful how and what you are asking for, if you choose to call or work with fae or other worldly energy).

Like with a garden, woods and forests shed and release so many magical ingredients that can be used in spell work. If you choose to take something, where possible always take something that has already been released as opposed to picking something from a plant that is living. Ask if it's OK in thought and also be thankful. If you ask and you feel it's not ok to take one of Mother Earth's treasures, make sure you put it back where you found it.

Often within the woods I come across all different types of fallen branches and - leaves, that can be used in spell work.

Trees you may encounter and their magical properties

Alder - *Birth of Spring* - The seasonal return of the Fae - PAN

Apple - *Tree of Life* - For health, vitality and wellbeing - IDUNA

Ash - *World Tree* - Holds all worlds in balance - ODIN

Aspen - *Tree of Courage* - Protection, facing one's fears - FRIGG

Beech - *Queen of The Woods* - Tolerance and compassion - ARTEMIS

Birch - *Lady of The Woods* - Ancestral spirits of the land - ELEN

Blackthorn - *Warrior Tree* - To defeat one's enemies - THOR

Hawthorn - *Tree of May* - Protection of loved ones - OLWEN

Hazel - *Tree of Wisdom* - Wisdom and knowledge - TALIESIN

Holly - *Yule King* - One's noble, eternal higher self - SATURN

Ivy - *Key to the Woods* - Friendships - DIONYSUS and BACCHUS

Mistletoe - *All Heal* - Essence of life and fertility - BALDER

Oak - *King of The Woods* - Strength and endurance - JUPITER

Pine - *Tree of Heights* - Aspirations and far seeing - DIONYSUS

Rose - *Tree of love* - For matters of heart and union - VENUS

Rowan - *Bright Spirit* - The fires of inspiration - BRIGHID

Willow - *Tree of Tears* - Heals the broken heart - HECATE

Yew - *Tree of Death* - For being with those who have died - HECATE

It doesn't just have to be woods or a forest to perform magick in. You may also find you have a suitable field area nearby with beautiful green unspoilt country-side. Or you may know of a hill area you like to walk up to. A personal favourite place for me when I visit Wiltshire, is the beautiful Avebury. The ancient stones can act as a magical altar. I also love Clay Hill on the edge of Warminster in Wiltshire. Known for recent crop circles in the field below the hill, and a popular sighting of UFOs. (If you are drawn to somewhere that may attract tourists, be mindful of when you choose to visit a location - to perform magick).

As well as the above, another beautiful space to work within is the magick of the water. You may know of a beautiful lake, stream or river area. Or you may have a favourite sandy beach you like to visit. The power of the sea can really strengthen and amplify magical spell work. There's nothing more beautiful then listening and watching - the waves crashing within the ocean and breathing in that mystical salty sea air. Again, early morning or later in the evening - can be perfect times to perform magick by the sea, as beaches tend to be more rural so you won't be disturbed. Often the tides wash in huge pieces of driftwood on the shore. Perfect for using as a mini altar whilst you create or perform a spell. Often feathers, seashells, hag stones and more can be found within a sandy beach.

All of the above can lend themselves to act as a perfect area to perform magick. There is no right or wrong place they are all powerful - and are all Mother Earth's temples. Depending on which spell you are needing may determine where you feel drawn to working. When we work in nature, we also work with the elements. Here is a mini breakdown that may help you when creating your own magick...

The Elements

Spirit - *the element of Centre or the self* - The Soul, The Divine, The Mystery

Air - *the element of the East* - Intuition, Knowledge, Renewal, Change

Water - *the element of the West* - Healing, Expression, Peace, Compassion

Fire - *the element of the South* - Passion, Inspiration, Intuition, Creativity, Protection

Earth - *the element of the North* - Fertility, Wealth, Abundance, Strength, Wisdom.

Once you have found a suitable location for you, your own magick can begin. I am blessed with a lovely garden area so tend to do a lot of my outdoor magick there. I have created a little altar area which is my-temple within my own garden. Often, I will get up early and sit in my garden with my morning coffee, and just spend time connecting and feeling blessed with what I have, and the beauty that surrounds me.

Here is the first basic spell I would like to share with you, I find this to be very simple but effective...

Morning Spell

To perform this spell, you will need your favourite mug of morning brew and the power of your intention.

Say in thought or out loud:

Bring More Magic To My Day

Take My Fears & Cares Away

Make Me Sparkly, Make Me Bright

Fill My Day With Living Light

Beauty's Love Revealed To Me

Luck & Joy & Ecstasy

Surprise, Success & Harmony

That's My Will, So Shall It Be!

*Those who don't believe in magic, will never find it -
Roald Dahl*

BASIC WITCH'S ALTAR

People sometimes ask me are altars needed, what's the point or purpose? It's entirely a personal choice if you choose to use an altar or not. It might be you call upon certain Deitys when practicing your magick. Some people like to dress their altars accordingly to honour the God and Goddess. Some people use an altar to honour the witches' wheel and the change in seasons and - again dress accordingly. The choices are endless...

In my home I have four altars that I use. I have two main altars for spell work and two other altars which are more just for show and honouring of the Deitys and spirit realm. My two main altars for doing spell work are my outside garden altar, and my witch's altar in my reading and treatment room. (My spare bedroom is done up as a therapy room - It sounds more grand than it is).

So, what is needed for a basic working altar? The purpose of the altar is an area you may wish to use to perform magick. Whilst it's lovely to have all the fancy kit it is optional. Often when I travel on the road with my spiritual work, I take a very basic travel altar with me.

Below are some options of things you may wish to have for a typical altar, and what you can use as an alternative...

The Tools

<u>The Athame</u> - A tool of the element Fire or Air. A double-edged ritual dagger traditionally with a black hilt used to cast circles of protection, banish negative energy, and charge and consecrate objects.

Alternatives - Can be a kitchen knife or blade, a letter opening knife, pen knife.

The Bell - A tool of invocation, bells are most often used to banish negative influences and for space clearing at the beginning of rituals.

Alternatives - You can get the cheap gimmick bells in the bargain shops and redecorate them to look more in keeping. Bells need not be costly. You may also have a singing bowl or alternative bells that you can use.

The Besom - A broom used to purify rituals and celebration areas by symbolically sweeping away negative energies. Besoms are also used to protect against negativity and psychic attacks. Some witches believe it's important to keep the besom upright with bristles up outside a home to ward off negative and unwanted energy.

Alternatives - If you haven't got access to a broom, you could also use a garden broom. Halloween is a great time of year as again must cheap shops sell a form of broomstick for a couple of quid. If you're crafty I would also encourage making your own. As you could have fun in the woods finding certain twigs and branches etc. to use. (YouTube is a great place to see how to make brooms if you fancy getting crafty).

The Cauldron - A tool of the element Water. A pot or vessel used in the making of brews and potions, and for the making of small fires for certain magical rites. Cauldrons can also be used for divination purposes and are a symbol of death and birth - Rebirth and the womb of the Goddess.

Alternatives - Cauldrons can range in many shapes and sizes. Growing up as a child I used my nan's big stew pot which made a perfect cauldron. You could also use a mug or coffee cup. As long as it can house liquid without leaking and is fire proof. Standard kitchen pots and pans can work just as well.

The Censer - A tool of the element of Air. A container, usually with a handle for ease in carrying, used to burn incense during rituals and celebrations.

Alternatives - Again mugs and cups can work just as well here, or even a little drinking glass.

The Chalice - A tool of the element of Water. Used to symbolize both containment and the womb of the Goddess. The chalice is also used to hold blessed water, libations or wine during rituals.

Alternatives - Chalices tend to be metal. However, a lovely wine glass works just the same.

The Pentacle - A tool of the element Earth. A round solid disk made from stone, wood or metal with a pentagram either craved into it or drawn onto it.

Alternatives - This is very easy to make and gives you the chance to be crafty. You could also visit a bead or fabric shop, as they often sell pentacle charms for a couple of quid if you haven't got time to make something yourself.

The Wand - A tool of the element of Fire or Air. A tool of invocation, wands are used to charge objects, bestow blessings, draw down the moon during rituals and celebrations, and to evoke the God and Goddess. Wands can be made of wood, glass, or various metals and are sometimes tipped on one or both ends with a crystal or gemstone. Copper wire is also sometimes wrapped around the point to enhance the spell work.

Alternatives - Any wand shaped branch you can find will work perfectly, try and identify where the tree branch has come from, as this will give you an idea of how that energy will work for you in spells. We also can use our power finger and point if you are not able to create a wand.

These are the basic tools needed to create an altar of your choice. By creating an altar within or around your home, you are actually making a sacred space for you spell work. This usually becomes a place that's important to you, where you are able to still your mind in order to allow yourself the freedom to express your own magick.

Now you may have an idea of how and where you are going to perform your workings, we can explore the power of spells. The spells I have included within this book are basic spells that can be done pretty much anywhere.

They are spells I have had to cast myself and use or I have done for people. Again, for me I prefer to keep my magick simple...

Days to Perform Magick -

Whilst there are no 'set in stone' rules to when you should or shouldn't cast a spell. There are some traditional ideas of when its preferable to perform certain types of magick. The below gives you a quick easy to understand break-down should you feel drawn to honouring the traditional ways...

Monday

This is the day of the Moon and traditionally washday. Monday is ideal for all magical work involving healing, intuition, dreamtime, development, health, fertility matters, and emotional being. Monday is also a good time to travel. Especially if this involves journeying over water.

Tuesday

This is the day of Mars, the planet of power and dynamism. It is a day for action, positive input, and creative energy. Tuesday is an ideal day for working on the resolution of conflicts, removal of relationship or family difficulties, issues of authority, justice and power.

Wednesday

The day of Mercury, the messenger. Ideal for working on all issues of communication, travel, study, and personal growth.

Thursday

The day of Jupiter, the planet associated with good fortune. Ideal for issues involving luck, employment, money and wealth, legal issues, and foreign matters.

Friday

The day of Venus. The tradition of eating fish on a Friday originated from the fact that fish are sacred for the love Goddess, and Friday is her sacred day. Ideal for spell weaving on relationship issues, harmony, friendships, marriage and creativity.

Saturday

The day of Saturn, the planet of limitation, time, and karma. Ideal for the removal of obstacles, limitations, or issues of personal understanding, legacies, property and land matters.

Sunday

This is the day of the Sun. It is an ideal time for all magical work associated with good health, money, prosperity and success.

I am the most powerful tool in my life and I will use ME Wisely - Author Unknown

MOON MAGICK

The Moon is a powerful, mysterious Mistress... how often have you gazed up at a full Moon, and been spellbound by her splendour and beauty? - How often have you felt in equal measure affected by her energy, drained? energised? lack of sleep? emotional wreck?...

The Moon is a powerful tool within spell casting and magick. By understanding the cycles of the Moon, we can tailor a spell to meet our requirements. Here is an easy to understand breakdown of the Moon phases and cycles...

New Moon

The new Moon phase runs from the first day after the dark Moon (when no Moon is seen in the sky) until the moon reaches its first quarter (when half the Moon is seen in the sky). During a new Moon is the perfect time to plan and prepare for new beginnings, to develop ideas, to wish for something to increase or grow, to plant seeds of change for your future. This is also the ideal time to plant seeds that flower above the ground.

Full Moon

The power time of the full Moon when emotions can be highly charged. It is the point of manifestation, so is an ideal time to manifest and visualize what you wish to bring in to your world. Seek a vision of what it is that you would like to manifest and meditate upon it with clarity during the full Moon phase. This is also the time to celebrate the Moon and perform a full Moon ceremony or ritual of thanks to her.

Waning Moon

The time of release and of harvest. This is the time to perform all healing rituals and spells of release, as well as drawing in any harvest from what you have achieved in this particular Moon's cycle. It is the time to cut back from whatever has not manifested yet, having first assessed what you have managed to achieve and considered what you now need to do to prepare for the coming new Moon. It is also the time to perform all banishing spells and rituals.

Dark Moon

The dark Moon is the one night in the Moon's cycle when there is no Moon in the sky. This is like the womb of creation, where there is potential for boundless disorder in thought, word, or deed. There are no restrictions in the void of the Moon, although a difficult energy to embrace or work with, it can offer invaluable insights during meditation or when seeking a vision. For working magick, it is not recommended. This particular night is best used for personal understanding and spiritual growth.

Moon Magick Spell - New Moon

To perform this spell, you will need the power of your intention:

Say in thought or out loud:

New Moon So Dark In The Night Sky

That Cannot Be Seen With Naked Eye

Grant Me Your Dark Energy To See

The New And Good Coming To Me

Grant Me The Power Of Dreams So True

So I Can Start My Life Anew

Grant Me Strength Day By Day

Mistress Of Darkness Show Me The Way

Grant Me love In My Life

Take Away Trouble And Strife

Grant Me Peace I Ask Of You

On Bad Times Help Me Through

O' Goddess Of Night So Divine

If You Have Heard Me Show Me A Sign

Moon Magick Spell - New Moon Broom Ritual

To perform this spell, you will need a besom/broom and the power of your intention:

Sweep with the broom in a circle motion and say in thought or out loud:

Sweep Out Evil, Sweep Out Ill

Where I Do The Lady's Will

Besom, Besom, Lady's Broom

Sweep Out Darkness, Sweep Out Doom

Witches Broom Swift In Flight

Cast Out Darkness, Bring In Light

Earth Be Hallow, Air Be Pure, Fire Burn

Bright, As Water Cures

A Sacred Bridge This Site Shall Be

As I Will, So Mote It Be

Moon Magick Spell - Full Moon Wish

To perform this spell, you will need some juice or wine in a chalice and the power of your intention:

At night, when the moon is full, go outside with a chalice of juice or wine. Look up at the Moon and tell it exactly what your heart desires (be specific). When you are done, lift your glass as a toast to the Moon and say in thought or out loud:

Mother Goddess, Look And See

This Chalice That I Offer Thee

It Is Yours For All you Do

Gracious One Of Silver View

Pour the juice or wine on the ground, and know your wish will be granted

Moon Magick Spell - Full Moon Ritual

To perform this spell, you will need the power of your intention.

Say in thought or out loud:

Moon Of Finest Silver Wane

Take Away Bad Luck And Pain

As You Fade Into The Night

Bring New Hope

Back In Sight

Moon Magick Spell - Waning Moon

To perform this spell, you will need the power of your intention:

Say in thought or out loud:

O Beautiful Moon Waning In Light

Nothing Compares To Your Beauty This Night

I Ask Thee Fair Crone To Take Away

Things That Do Not Serve Me In A Positive Way

Take The Things That Stop My Growth

So I Can Serve Thee, It Is My Oath

Remove The Things I No Longer Need

So I Can prepare Anew, For This I Plead

Make Me New For The Dark Moon Phase

I Ask This Great Crone For The Coming Days

Blessed Be

Moon Magick Spell - Waning Moon Ritual

To perform this spell, you will need the power of your intention.

Say in thought or out loud:

Cleanse and Clear

The Moon Whispers To

Let Go Of Your Pain and Fears

The Time Has Come To Go Within

Reflect and Learn From

Where You've Been
The Sky Is Growing Darker
Each Passing Night
Inviting You To Tend To
Your Own Inner Light
Trust In The Divine
And Set Yourself Free
So Mote It Be
So Mote It Be

Moon Magick Spell - Dark Moon Ritual

To perform this spell, you will need the power of your intention.

Say in thought or out loud:

Dark Moon Prayer
Ancient Wise One, Wayfarer Of The Night
Take All That Has To End
All That Must Disappear And Die With You
Into The Darkness
I Welcome Your Peace, I Welcome The Stillness
As You Disappear Into The Dawn
So I Choose To Go Within
Blessed Be

I'll ask the Moon, before I sleep, let this love be mine to keep for always. This was the moment the magick began, I wish I may, I say I can.... - Lucie Arnaz

PROTECTION MAGICK

I wanted to start off with this area of spell work, as it's very important to know how to protect yourself and your home against unwanted or undesired energy. Unfortunately, this is an area I seem to have had quite a few dealings and personal experience with.

As I said at the start of this book, I neither work with Black or White magick... I work with the magick that's required for the highest of good at a certain time. Depending on the situation I will channel and spell cast what is needed.

It's important to explain that as with anything in this world there is good and bad. Not everyone whom works in the spiritual circles, are truly spiritual. What I mean by that is some people portray them self to work for the light, but that is just a mask they wear. Sadly, underneath the surface, there may be an uglier darker version, of the true reflection of that person. Living a spiritual walk of life is both in front of people, and behind closed doors.

Surely not?... you may be wondering? Sadly so... How do I know? I've seen this first hand on numerous occasions and been the victim of others' lower energy. People portray themselves a certain way and talk a good game, but remember actions always speak louder than words. Work with the seen and unseen eye. Perhaps this is one of the reason's - why I am now for the most part a solitary witch. Too many people have seemed to misplace my trust in them - or abused a friendship or a working relationship. Often in books this isn't talked about. If you spend time watching and being aware of people's energy, you will uncover the truth, and unmask those on a lower vibration. As I said before, often this doesn't get talked about... so people stay blind-folded and unable to see the truth. But it is time to be aware, and to wake up, if you yourself have been in a slumber.

...Darkness does not always equate to evil...Light does not always bring good...

Sometimes through no fault of our own, when we become good, or even successful at something, for some unknown reason! people around us may start to change. Some will celebrate and be happy and genuinely wish you well in all you do. Be blessed you have these gems within your network of people. But be mindful of others, as others will say they are happy for you, but inside you may feel a coldness or negative energy being directed towards you. Pay attention to how your gut is feeling. Gut feelings never lie...

Some people are unable to wish others well. They may feel threatened or worried that someone, in their eyes is becoming more successful than them self. Never ever apologise for investing the time into you. When you are truly connected with self, you have absolutely no need to worry about what anyone else is or isn't doing around you. Dance to the rhythm and power of your own magick. Don't let these types of people project their own fear on to you, as it is not a reflection of the truth, it's a limitation they are trying to place upon you.

Through my mediumship work, it has definitely exposed the good, the bad, and the downright ugly. I have been a victim on numerous occasions of psychic attacks and even hexes. But why? Was there a reason? It's important to not judge a book by its cover. Often when we see someone doing well, we may automatically think 'wow they've got it made'. We create a preconceived idea of how their world may be. But no one knows what might be going on behind closed doors or underneath the surface. I have spent a lot of time investing in me, this isn't something that has a time-frame to it. This is a lifelong ongoing personal journey. To be better to myself than I was yesterday. At times this has been a tough, hard, painful journey. People sometimes allow the green–eyed monster out, and that's when jealous or envious nature creeps in. For me, these are both wasted emotions, they serve no purpose. They cause hurt, drama, damage and unwanted problems. If you yourself are feeling this way towards a person or situation. Stop and ask why, why would you be allowing someone's success to block your own? I am a firm believer in not allowing people or situations to have power over another. We get back out of this world what we choose to put in. Invest wisely and check on what direction your own moral compass is pointing.

PSYCHIC ATTACKS

For me psychic attacks are a real low blow. You have to be a little bit messed up in the head in my opinion, to choose to send someone hurtful or negative energy. This is exactly what a psychic attack is. In your mind's eye you are choosing to project energy, that can hinder, harm or block that person.

It sounds all a bit dramatic but psychic attacks really are not fun to experience. They can also happen in the unlikeliest of circumstances. I was doing a demonstration of mediumship when I first realised I had been psychically attacked, the very first time it happened. People paid money to come and watch me, only to then try and block me. Doesn't make sense really does it? Sadly, this is a lot more common than you might think. The 'wanna be' mediums who may not have been good enough to serve on platform, so they waste their time blocking and trying to trip people up en route. Thankfully I am blessed with an amazing strong spirit team, of guides, angels and helpers. So, the night continued with no problems. However, it was the days after I knew something was wrong. Imagine when you are maybe a little drunk or hungover, that feeling of helplessness, stuck in your bed. Too weak to move for fear of being sick, the room spinning a million miles an hour. That was the feeling I had for almost a week after. My mentor at the time realised what had happened, and through various exercises I was able to remove the attack and I started to feel normal again. It took almost another week to rebuild my strength, my third eye chakra at the time felt like it had blown up.

What did they gain from projecting that towards me, and stopping me in my tracks for two weeks? very little... I view this experience as a lesson for me... as moving forward it certainly made me up my level of protection.

<u>So, what should you look out for, if you feel you are being psychically attacked?...</u>

- Power loss - Your body may feel weak, almost like it has no energy, and you may feel faint or pass out.

- Extreme fatigue or tiredness - You may feel like your body just wants to sleep, and you may have to sleep during the day for long periods of time.

- Headaches or migraines - You may feel pain within the third eye or crown chakra, as after all you are being blocked from connecting. This can range from pressure around the temples to full blown migraines.

- Mindset - You may feel extremely angry, confrontational, frustrated, negative for no real reason at all. Check how you are behaving and coming across, are you being yourself?

- Appetite - You may go long periods of not wanting to eat or drink, again be mindful if this is out of character.

- Hostile - You may feel moody with friends, family, work colleagues or clients around you, and be snapping out people with no reason.

- Hurting - You may feel extremely emotional or the body may feel in physical pain

- Blocks - You may feel if you work spiritually that you have a mental block and, are unable to get links of any kind psychic or mediumship for people. You will feel unable to do a reading or give any evidence.

Hexes

Hexes work very similar to psychic attacks and are in my eyes a misuse of magick. I have sadly also been a victim of hexes. The symptoms are very similar to those of a psychic attack, but also hexes can draw in bad luck or misfortune to a person. They can create illusion where friends and family turn against you. To me to hex a person is very dangerous and you have little to no control over what the victim might experience and be subjected to.

It's <u>NOT</u> OK for witches to go around throwing hexes because they feel they can or are somehow entitled too. It's a complete misuse of power and magick in my eyes.

I had a really bad hex placed on me from a "so - called White Witch", I have a rescue dog called Oscar who is a very damaged boy. Me and my partner have been trying various things to give him his quality of life back. It's often said people hurt us through the ones we love the most. This particular White Witch for reasons, I still am unsure of today, took a dislike to me. I think it may have been again an envious reason, but I will never fully know. She decided to hex both myself but also, my Jack Russell, Oscar. Now... it's one thing to hex a person! but to hex a defenceless animal? that is pure evil. The result was Oscar constantly wanting to attack me. Often, he would lunge at me with his fangs out, blood shot eyes, it was like when I was looking at him he was cold, dead behind the eyes almost possessed. Certainly not my boy. There in the physical sense - but lost in mental state.

This continued for nearly two months, he would be fine with my partner but pure evil to me. I knew in my gut something was wrong. The vets were concerned from a safety aspect and suggested he may need to be put to sleep. It was a trying time and nearly broke my relationship with my partner, it felt like we were arguing night and day, trying to make sense and understand just what was going on, and why he was acting this way. I knew in my heart of hearts this was not my boy. Whilst Oscar has extreme fear aggression amongst other things, this felt altogether different. Through the grapevine I was made aware of a similar experience that someone else had been put through, by the same so called "White Witch". Their cat had turned against them and gone feral. They knew this was a hex so did a spell to break it. As soon as they performed this spell all the problems stopped.

I suddenly understood what had happened to me and Oscar. I have a few close witch friends whom I trust 110%. I confided in them and through their help they confirmed it was a hex and were able to break this spell. They too were shocked that an animal had been used to hurt someone, the lowest of the low. As soon as the hex was lifted stillness and waves of unconditional love filled the house once more. Oscar was embracing me as he had always done before and started being affectionate as if nothing had happened. I can never forgive this person for doing such damage to my boy. It could have cost him his life - And me my relationship. Was this the desired outcome the "White Witch" wanted? I will never truly know. But I am so blessed to have powerful friends that were able to help me undo such evil.

Here are some basic powerful protection spells below, and spells to undo and break a hex:

Protection Spell - Black Candle

To perform this spell, you will need 1 black candle, a mirror, and the power of your intention.

If you feel influenced by negative energies, light a black candle in front of a mirror and say out loud:

Any Dark Or Evil Force

May Now Return To Its Source

May My Home And I Be Free

Safe And Well - So Mote It Be

Protection Spell - White Light

To perform this spell, you will need the power of your intention.

Imagine rings of pure white light circling around you within your mind's eye and say in thought or out loud:

Three Times The Rings Go Around

All Evil Shall Stay On The Ground

If Any Evil Is Near This Place

It Cannot Enter My Sacred Space

Three Times Three

So Mote It Be!

Protection Spell - Banish Bad Luck

To perform this spell, you will need the power of your intention.

Chant as many times as needed, in your thoughts or out loud:

Today Is Not My Day

Everything Has Gone Astray

To Keep Me Sane

To Keep The Peace

Bad Luck Coming My Way Shall Cease

I Banish Pain

I Banish Sorrow

Gods And Goddesses Bless My Tomorrow

Protection Spell - Release Negative Energy

To perform this spell, you will need a piece of paper, a pen, a fire and the power of your intention.

Write down on a piece of paper, any people, situations, experiences you want to release and say the following in thought or out loud, then throw the paper into a burning fire:

Mother Earth Hear My Call...

The Time For Change Is Set About For All

See My List, Hear My Plea,

Send This Unwanted Energy Far Away From Me

Clear My Aura, Cleanse My Soul

Detach The Energies That Have Gained Control

No Harm I Cause, I Send With Love

That's My Will, So Mote It Be

Protection Spell - Egg Shell Magick

To keep an unwanted person or visitor away from your home with some grounded egg shell.

To perform this spell, you will need some grounded egg shell and the power of your intention.

Sprinkle the egg shell at the front of your door, when the unwelcome person has left, say in thought or out loud:

May I See You Know More

You Are Not Welcome At My Door

Go Away & Let Me Be

On Your Way, Give Me Piece

You Are Not Welcome Anymore

Stay Away From My Door

Protection Spell - For Your Family and Loved Ones

To perform this spell, you will need a white candle, incense of your choice, photos of loved ones and your family, and the power of your intention.

Light the incense, place the candle in the middle with your photos around it. Light the candle and visualise a beautiful white protection circle around all you hold dear, say in thought or out loud:

O Goddess, Protect My Loved Ones Every Day

As They Sleep As They Play

Help Them To Always Smile Bright

And Keep Them Safe In Your loving light
Protect Them From harm
And All They Fear
For They Are The Ones That I hold Dear
I Thank The Goddess For Helping Me
I Trust In Her Aid
So Mote It Be

Protection Spell - To Break A Hex

To perform this spell, you will need three candles (these could be tea lights or spell candles) and the power of your intention.

Light the three candles in a triangle and then say the following in thought or out loud:

Break This Spell, Break This Curse
By Three Candles, By End Of Verse
Reflect Back Three Times Three
Your Hex Has No Affect On Me
Curse Return By Candles Three
Burn Away And Set Me Free
Live And Learn, Crash And Burn
Three Times Three This Hex Return!
As I Will It. So Mote It Be!

Protection Spell - Curse or Hex Reversal

To perform this spell, you will need two candles, preferably black, black salt and the power of your intention.

Perform outside, create a ring or protection circle of black salt. Light two black candles and then chant in thought or out loud:

In The Name Of The Gods & Goddesses And All The Spirits

In The Name Of Kernunnos & Hecate And The Light And The Dark

And The Gods Of The Netherworld And Whosoever Shall Be Casting A Curse Against

...(Victim's Name)...

Let Them Suffer Their Own Curse

Let These Candles Be Their Candles

This Burning Be Their Burning

This Curse Be Their Curse

Let The Pain They Have Caused ...(Victim's Name)...

And Theirs Fall Upon Themselves

This Is My Will So Mote It Be

Blessed Be

Blessed Be

Blessed Be

Let both candles burn down fully to complete this spell. You may find a candle or candle holder splits or breaks. This will indicate the spell has worked and been undone.

I also wanted to include a couple of quick and easy spells for our fur babies...

Protection Spell - Blessings Spell for Dogs

To perform this spell, you will need the power of your intention.

Say in thought or out loud:

Diana, Goddess of The Wild

Keeper Of Dogs Both Fierce And Mild

Hold ...(Name Of Pet)... Safely In Your Arms

And Protect This Creature From All Harm

And Should The Day Come That (He/She) Roams

Guide (Him/Her) To The Path Back Home

Bless ...(Name Of Pet)... With A Joyful Life

Free Of Hardship, Stress And Strife.

Protection Spell - Blessings Spell for Cats

To perform this spell, you will need the power of your intention.

Say in thought or out loud:

Beast Of Beauty And Of Grace

Protectress Of The Feline Race

Shield ...(Name Of Pet)... From All Hurt And Harm

And Keep (Him/Her) Always Safe And Warm

Watch Over ...(Name Of Pet)... From Day To Day

And Guide (Him/Her) Home If (He/She) Should Stray

And Grant (Him/Her) Much Happiness

And A Good Life Free Of Stress And Strife.

Confidence isn't walking into a room thinking you are better than everyone; it's walking in not having to compare yourself to anyone at all. - Author Unknown

BANISHMENT AND BINDING MAGICK

From time to time you have probably had somebody around you that has tried to make life difficult. The situation at hand maybe pretty straight forward or easy. Yet this type of person seems determined on making matters difficult for you. This could be within your working world or through landlords, family, friends, neighbours or home life. It's not that they are bad people, they may not even be aware how their actions and behaviours have made you feel. Or it could be they are aware but are choosing to carry on regardless.

Banishment spells are different to the above I have shared with you so far. They still protect your energy, but they shift the unwanted energy along. This is done in love and light so no hurt or harm will come to that person.

I wanted to share with you an experience I had, the first time I needed to use a spell of this nature. Before I did my mediumship work full time... I worked in very aggressive sales and advertising company. The corporate world can be a scary place for an awakened soul. My own personal experience of the corporate world wasn't particularly pleasant. A world fueled by mainly masculine energy, arrogance, greed, ego, and manipulation. I'm sure that there are maybe good parts within some companies. But sadly, I didn't see this in the company I worked for, for over 7 years.

This situation must have been in the last couple of months before I left that company. For a time I was acting manager. The manager that had been in the business, had been asked to leave with immediate effect. The assistant manager had been sacked for fraud and gross misconduct. So already things were in a bit of mess. I was the acting manager and keeping the team and the store I worked in afloat until a new manger was assigned. This suited me fine as I had absolutely no desires to progress within the company. I had worked as assistant manager before and had been manager in other jobs, I could easily live without it.

A new manager was assigned. A middle aged, potbellied, bald, Scottish man. For the purposes of this book we will call him Mr A... A for Arsehole...as this is exactly what he was. Within the first few days it was clear that we were not going to be friends. I respected him in his position as manager, but I had no respect for him as a person. Think of him as a Scottish bald headed Donald Trump! He viewed himself as something special, a cut above everybody else and he was manager so what he said was fact. The problem was he had his head stuck so far up his own backside, he couldn't understand and struggled to get to grips with the actual job in hand. You have to gain respect, it's not just given to you because of your title. He seemed to fail to understand this from the off.

Over the coming months, I had to try and teach him the ropes and for him to get to grips with the job. We faced countless problems, he seemed very bad at following basic instructions himself and he would blow hot headed over the smallest of things. The longer I spent time with him the more, he made my skin crawl. Not only was he useless in his job as manager, he fancied himself as something special. Often with female clients he would believe that they were flirting with him. I've never seen someone twist the truth so quick, but also he was believing the bullshit he was saying. It was seriously cringe worthy. He also would often bring up my sexuality, life-style choices, and spiritual followings. These subjects where off limits and I certainly wouldn't be sharing those personal details with the likes of this Scottish muggle.

Time went on and we seemed to be getting nowhere fast. A lovely mentor I had at the time made me aware of a quick and easy banishment spell. She seemed shocked I hadn't come across it before. The truth of the matter was, I had never even thought to use magick within my working world. Had I done this sooner I may have not gone through so much garbage. Although I am a firm believer in everything happens for a reason, and I do believe Mr A came in to teach me lessons of some kind. Even if it was just to highlight that my own moral compass was pointing in the right direction.

I didn't cast the spell immediately... I thought I would hold fire and see if things got better. Sadly, they never did. Sometimes with magick we get pushed to a point where we run out of other options. It was clear that Mr A was quite happy with himself, in his eyes he saw himself as perfect, untouchable, he was however... disrespectful to women, homophobic, and racist. I'd had more than enough of his smallminded ways, it was time for him to go...

I decided to cast the spell... wow... I've never had a spell work so quickly for me. Within 2 days!!! of casting the spell sure enough, the problem was being shifted along with love and light. The powers that be higher up in the company, for no reason at all, decided to transfer him to another branch with immediate effect. This was completely out of the blue and off the cuff unexpected - Mr A travelled from Swindon each day to Trowbridge in Wiltshire. There was not a position in Swindon however, so they decided he needed to be there until further notice. They made it clear this wasn't permanent but for now. This worked a treat... as it allowed me to then carry on working in peace and harmony once more. Until the time came that I felt ready to leave the company for good. The remaining time I was there I had no dealings with him. Mr A was out of my life for good. It felt good flushing the biggest turd down the loo...

I want to share with you this spell, and a few others, you can try if you have to banish a person or a situation out of your life. Remember to always perform this with the intention of love. As these people do not need hurtful energy, sent their way. They need the vibration of love to heal themselves and in time correct their own behaviours and actions.

Banishment Spell - Freezer Spell

To perform this spell, you will need a pen and paper, a freezer, the power of your intention.

Write down on a piece of paper the situation, person, or people you wish to banish from your life. Fold the piece of paper in half, and then in half again. Send the feelings of the unwanted behaviours and energy into the paper. Then say in thought or out loud:

Great White Spirit, Hear My Call

Send This Person Away, Affect Me No More

I Wish Them Love, I Wish Them Health, I Banish Them Away

They Need Not Hurt Me, They Have No Power, Allow The Ice To Freeze The Matter

No Tears Are Caused, No Loss Of Sleep,

Days Are Gentle, I Find Release & Welcome In... My Own Awakened Inner Peace

With Harm To None. This Is My Will, There It Is Done. So Mote It Be

Then place the piece of paper into the freezer and leave it there, until the issue has become completely resolved. This will then literally freeze the problem. Once you have completely rid this issue out of your life, you may burn the piece of paper. This symbolises that issue never being able to control or hinder you again.

(Helpful tip - some people like to also dip or soak the paper in water or vodka before its frozen. I don't but it's your choice if you wish to do this. Some people also wrap their piece of paper in black cotton. The black symbolizes protection. Again, I don't but you can tailor the spell to your own personal requirements).

Banishment Spell - Hand Held Mirror

To perform this spell, you will need a handheld mirror, a photo of the person, or pen and paper to write down the intention of person or situation you wish to banish, sticky tape or black ribbon, and the power of your intention.

Place the photo or piece of paper of the person or situation face down onto the mirror. Start wrapping the tape or ribbon around the mirror, to keep it stuck onto the mirrors face. Whilst doing this say in thought or out loud:

Magick Mirror Within My Hand, Lock In The Poison Of Others Demands...

You And Your Negativity Will Stay Far Away From Me...

This Is My Will. So Mote It Be!

This will both keep them from you, and make sure their negativity is reflected away from you and back to them. You can if you like keep the mirror hidden away or bury it within the earth.

Banishment Spell - Bind A Troublemaker

To perform this spell, you will need a cauldron, three black candles, (if you have them herbs - sage, basil, elderflower) a wand, pen and paper to write down the name of people or situations and the power of your intention.

For best results perform this spell on a Waning Moon. Situate your cauldron between two black candles, with a third black candle opposite you on the far side of the altar.

Burn sage or a protection incense blend which you can make yourself. Have the names of the people you wish to bind and banish written down. Sprinkle basil, sage and elderflower into the cauldron whilst saying:

Bubble, Bubble, Cauldron Bubble

Burn The Evil, Destroy The Trouble

Ignite the piece of paper from the central candle and drop into the cauldron. Take up the wand (or point with your power finger) and stir the air above the cauldron while chanting.

Darkness Ended, Control Is Done

Light Has Come, My Battle's Won

Take the ashes and herbs outside, throw them up to the Winds and the Moon. Allow the elements to carry away the unwanted energy.

Banishment Spell - Remove A Toxic Person or Situation

To perform this spell, you will need three black candles, a photo of the person to banish, or a piece of paper with their name on, and the power of your intention.

Light three black candles in a triangle with the photo of the person that you want to banish, or a piece of paper with their name on, then say in thought or out loud:

Banish You Once, I Banish You Twice

I Banish You Right Out Of My Life

You Are Not Worth My Time

Stay Out Of My Life

No Need To Fight

I Said My Good Byes

So Mote It Be!

Keep the candles lit for one hour. Then snuff out the candles and bury all three black candles and the photo or piece of paper, far away from your home.

Don't compare your life to others. There's no comparison between the sun and the moon. They shine when it's their time. - Author Unknown

ABUNDANCE AND PROSPERITY MAGICK

From time to time we all get worried about money. We shouldn't but the human side of us does. It's always important to remember when we are in these money block cycles, by thinking of the negative its actually attracting that back into our world. The mind is like a magnet and like attracts like. So, if you are having money blocks always keep your thought patterns positive and moving forward (even if you may not feel this way). Of course, this can be easier said than done, but in time this becomes easier to master.

I wanted to share with you some simple abundance spells that have worked for me, when I have been in tricky situations. Remember often witches are blessed with riches far more magical than anything money can buy.

Abundance Spell - Friday the 13th

To perform this spell, it must be done on a Friday the 13th only of a month, you will need thirteen pennies, and the power of your intention.

Say in thought or out loud:

Today I Cast For Money Luck

As It Is Lucky, It Will Work Today

With These Pennies, I Display

The Money Is On The Way

The 13th Is Lucky

On The Witches Day

These 13 Pennies, Will Bring It My Way

This Will Harm None In Anyway

As It Is Lucky, If Done On This Day

Then bury the thirteen pennies into the earth, and allow the abundance to enter your world.

Abundance Spell - To Obtain Money

To perform this spell, this needs to be on a Full Moon you will need a silver coin of choice, a cauldron, some water, and the power of your intention.

Fill your cauldron half full of water and drop a silver coin into it. Position the cauldron so that the light from the Moon shines into the water. Gently sweep your hands just above the surface, symbolically gathering the Moon's silver.

Whilst doing this say in thought, or out loud:

Lovely Lady Of The Moon

Bring To Me Your Wealth Right Soon

Fill My Hands With Silver And Gold

All You Give, My Purse Can Hold

Then leave the cauldron outside overnight, and allow the abundance to enter your world.

Abundance Spell - Cinnamon Money Spell

To perform this spell, you will need a green candle, six coins of choice, a green pouch or piece of cloth, cinnamon, and the power of your intention.

Create a circle with the coins around the candle. Light the candle and say in thought or out loud three times:

Money Flow

Money Grow

Money Shine

Money Mine!

Sprinkle the bag or cloth with cinnamon and collect the coins and place them inside, while doing this say:

Bring me money 3 x 3

Keep the pouch or cloth with you for a while, until the abundance comes in for you.

Abundance Spell - Prosperity

To perform this spell, you will need the power of your intention.

Say in thought or out loud:

Money Money Come To Thee

Bless My Life With Prosperity

An Abundance To Share

An Abundance For Me

Magical Universe

Hear My Plea

With Harm To None

Including Me

This Is My Wish

So Blessed Be

Money is numbers and numbers never end. If it takes money to be happy, your search for happiness will never end - Robert Nesta Marley

KNOT MAGICK

This is my favourite type of magick to perform as it's simple but very powerful. You can literally do Knot Magick almost anywhere. You can tailor a spell to suit your own needs. I am blessed to have a small friendship circle of local witches near where I live. On occasion we meet at a secret sacred location. Where we chat about all things magical, drink home brew underneath the stars, relax around a roaring fire with the cauldron bubbling away, and now and again perform a spell or two...

One of my lovely best witch friends introduced me to the power of knot magick on one of are mystical nights. If you feel drawn to this style of magic you will need an old piece of string, shoelace, ribbon, cord, or anything else you may have lying around that you can use tie knots into. This type of magick is particularly handy if you travel around a lot and need something quick to use to spell cast.

Knot Spell - Manifestation

To perform this spell, you will need a piece of string or cord, a fire and the power of your intention.

Think of your intentions, ask your spirit guides, angels and helpers, Deitys (if you work with them) to lend strength to your manifestations. Imagine the string or cord absorbing all of these wishes and desires.

Then take your piece of string or cord and place knots into the string whilst you say in thought or out loud:

By Knot Of 1 The Spells Begun

By Knot Of 2 My Words Be True

By Knot Of 3 I Call To Thee

By Knot Of 4 My Words Are Lore

By Knot Of 5 So May It Thrive

By Knot Of 6 This Spell I Fix

By Knot Of 7 Events Will Leaven

By Knot Of 8 I Meld With Fate

By Knot Of 9 What's Done Is Mine

So Mote It Be, With Harm To None...

Now place your string into the fire and allow your thoughts to ignite into all your heart desires. (This spell is often also called or known as "The Witches Ladder")

Knot Spell - Knot Your Troubles

To perform this spell, you will need a piece of string or cord at least twelve inches long and the power of your intention.

You can use this spell no matter what your problem is. If you choose to use a coloured piece of string or cord, to symbolise your purpose, you can fine—tune the spell to your particular situation.

Hold the piece of string or cord with one end in each hand and pull it taught. Think about your problem. Concentrate on your difficult situations and start tying knots in the string. Visualise all your troubles getting bound up in the knots and trapped there. Keep tying as many knots as is needed until you feel all hurts are trapped.

Then take your piece of string and bury it within the earth to ground the energy - and keep the problems at bay.

Knot Spell - Basic Love Spell

To perform this spell, you will need three different coloured cords or strings and the power of your intention.

Take three cords or strings of various pastel colours like pink, yellow, and lilac and braid them. Firmly tie a knot near one end of the braid thinking of your need for love. Next tie another knot and another, until you have tied seven knots.

Wear or carry the cord or string with you until you find your love. After that, keep the cord in a safe place or give to one of the elements, burn it and toss the ashes into a stream.

When you reach the end of your rope, tie a knot in it and hang on - Thomas Jefferson

SELF HEALING MAGICK

Self-healing is a powerful journey of its own... I am a Reiki and Violet Flame Healer. From learning these forms of energy work I have been able to clear - many hurts from the past. It's not until you go on a healing journey of awakening, that you realise how much garbage and junk is stored up within our own heads and hearts. Many times I felt I had made my piece with situations I had been put into. But from doing my own Reiki work, what I discovered was that these situations had been suppressed. I hadn't actually rid myself of the energy attachments surrounding the situation. If you have never experienced the power of healing via Reiki or other types of healing, I would definitely encourage you to seek out a local practitioner in your area, and give it a try. You may be surprised at how reiki energy can cleanse and touch your soul.

The spells in this section of the book focus on how I used to be in my younger days. I hadn't experienced the power of reiki back then, if I had I think it would have really helped me. These spells I have felt drawn to sharing, and these are the spells I would offer the younger version of me to do. The child within that went through hurts, pains and feelings of overwhelming emotions. You may be feeling a certain way yourself right now, and you may feel drawn to a particular spell within this section. Self-healing magick as with anything else we have looked at so far, is a personal journey. Always allow the love to flow and enter into your own sacred heart. Know and trust it's OK to start with you, and look after yourself before others...

Self-Healing Spell - Self - Esteem Boost Spell

To perform this spell, you will need the power of your intention.

Say in thought or out loud:

I Am Intelligent And Can Succeed In All That I Wish

I Will Speak Clearly, I Will Speak Calmly

I Will Focus Only On The Positive In All Things Around Me Today

I Will Not Be Shaken

I Am Intelligent And Can Succeed In All That I Wish...

Self-Healing Spell - Be At Peace With Self

To perform this spell, you will need a mirror and the power of your intention.

Stand in front of a mirror and say in thought or out loud:

You Know What?

I Like Myself

I Trust Myself

I Know Myself

I Know What I Want

I Know What I Need

I Know What I Have

I Know What I Know

I Mean Well

I Try Hard

I Do Good

I Help

I Heal

I Hear

I Love

I Feel

I Fall Down

I Stand Up

I Strive

I Survive

I Flourish

I Thrive

Self-Healing Spell - Confidence

To perform this spell, you will need a yellow candle, a shell, and the power of your intention.

Light a yellow candle, holding it in your dominant hand and say in thought or out loud:

Please Give Me Confidence So I Can Be The Best

I Failed It Once But Now I Will Be Better Than The Rest

Pass the shell through the flame and say:

May This Be My Lucky Charm So My Wish Can Come True

Kiss the shell for good luck and pass it through the flame one last time and say:

May My Charm Help Me In All I Do

Self-Healing Spell - Confidence Ritual

To perform this spell, you will need a candle of choice and the power of your intention.

Light your candle and focus on the flame, and say to yourself or out loud:

Earth Below, Sky Above

Fill The Dark Of Night With Love

The Morning Sun Will Take My Pain

And I Will Wake Renewed Again

The Time Has Come

Renewed By Sun

To Count My Blessings One By One

Self-Healing Spell - Anxiety and Fear

To perform this spell, you will need the power of your intention.

Say in thought or out loud:

Anxiety And Fear Fills Me With Dread

Consuming Thoughts Must Go Be Dead

Our Lord And Lady Now Soothes My Head

Leaving Calm And An Eternal Peace

So Mote It Be This Is Released

Self-Healing Spell - Release Anger

To perform this spell, you will need a black crystal or stone, perform the spell near running water and the power of your intention.

Hold the black crystal or stone in your hand. Raise it to your forehead, concentrate and place all your anger into the stone or crystal. Do this until you can do it no longer. Throw your crystal or stone into moving, running water and say in thought or out loud:

With This Stone

Anger Be Gone

Water Bind It

No One Find It

Self-Healing Spell - To Banish Depression

To perform this spell, you will need a yellow and pink candle and the power of your intention.

Light both yellow and pink candles in front of you and say the following in thought or out loud:

Blessed Goddess Of Love And Light

Please Come Help Me On This Night

My Heart Is Heavy And My Feelings Are Blue

My Soul Is Sad I Don't Know What To Do...

Help Me Banish The Pain I Feel

This Lacklustre Feeling Has No Appeal

Help Me See The Love Begin And
Feel My Heart Be Light Again
Let Me Climb Up From This Hole
And Be With You Heart, Body And Soul
I Ask Thee Goddess On This Night Please
Help Me Make Myself Alright!
So Mote It Be

Self-Healing Spell - To Deal With Grief

To perform this spell, you will need a smoky quartz crystal, a bowl of water, three tablespoons of sea salt, and the power of your intention.

Begin by holding the stone in your power hand. See your grief in your mind's eye. Visualise the grief moving from within yourself and through your hand to the stone.

Say in thought or out loud:

Banishing Stone
Fill Yourself With My Grief
So That I May Feel Joy Again
So Be It, Blessed Be!

Stirring anticlockwise, mix the sea salt into the bowl of water then add the smoky quartz crystal. Swish the stone around three times in an anticlockwise motion. Leave the stone in the water for a few minutes then take the stone outside and safely throw it as far as you can away from you.

Self-Healing Spell - Healing

To perform this spell, you will need the power of your intention.

Say in thought or out loud:

By Earth & Air

By Fire & Water

So Shall You Hear My Call

Powers Of Birth & Rebirth

Powers Of Silence & Peace

Heal My Body & My Mind

Self-Healing Spell - To Stop Judgement

To perform this spell, you will need the power of your intention.

Say in thought or out loud:

I Cast This Spell So You Will See

Your Hurtful Words & Judging Me

The Expectations You Place On Me

Cause Harmful Negativity

Your Standards Place Only On your Self

Not Others As It Harms Their Health

I Pray That Only Blessed Be

Your Judgmental Ways You Now See

Treat Others Only In The Way you Wish To Be Treated

Or You Yourself May Well Become Defeated

Your Judgements Do Not Affect Me Now
The Goddess Has Healed And Shown Me How
Live With Love & Accepting Ways
And Forever Live Only Happy Days
So Mote It Be

DREAD WITCH

I wanted to share with you an experience that happened to me. From as young as I can remember I had always wanted dread locks. I felt like within the soul of my being this is how I saw my witchy self with my psychic eye. I have always felt that my clean, smart appearance was never 100% me, and below the surface there was a more earthy image that needed in time release. Through most of my adult life before becoming a full time light worker, I worked for companies where dread-locks were simply a no go, and completely off limits.

However, in early February 2018, I was introduced to someone who made and installed dreadlocks. Like the never-ending layers of an onion, I felt like I was peeling back, and healing and exposing the raw version of who I truly was. Now successfully working for myself, I had no one else to tell me what was and wasn't deemed acceptable. With that in mind, I booked myself in to have a beautiful set of dread-locks made and installed.

Everything was perfect. I loved my new look, I felt like I had turned my body inside out. How I felt on the inside, my physical outside image now matched. Over the months I enjoyed adding various crystals, beads and witchy charms into my hair. I felt the beads and charms almost told a story.

I was enjoying life as a dread witch... I felt whole and complete. Another deeper layer of self-healing I felt. This was however... also a period of time where I seemed to receive a lot of negative and envious energy around me. There was no rhyme or reason for it?... but you know what they say there's nothing more weirder than folk!

As time went on I was having to perform many protection and release spells. Around the middle of July-2018, I was really feeling the heat. We had been blessed with a gorgeous summer, the hottest on record for years. I thought the heat might finish me off, but weirdly it didn't seem to worry me too much at all.

Something had changed though. I suddenly felt very low, tired and no energy. I started to dislike how I saw myself and was feeling incredibly drained. Suddenly out of the blue, the dreads I had wanted for years, seemed to not be sitting so well with me. Whilst they still looked perfect, almost as if overnight, they were bugging me, and I literally wanted to rip them one by one off my head.

I decided I needed to meditate on this... It didn't seem right to all most turn on something I had wanted for so long. Through the power of meditation, I connected with my female spirit guide Solara. (who also has partial dreads). She showed me all the spells, all the releasings and what was happening. Suddenly as if a light had been switched on it all made sense. Where I had been releasing, healing and letting go of toxic energy, my real hair was shedding. The problem was my dreads where synthetic hair extensions, that wrapped and were installed around my real hair. The fake hair was collecting all the garbage and junk, and stale and negative energy. It became clear what I had to do.

The coming days I decided to book in to have the extensions out. Whilst I was waiting I couldn't be seen till nearly the end of the month. One day I literally just had enough, with the help of my mum we cut the dreads out. She tried to salvage the remaining hair, but it had become quite bad, so we decided to shave it all off.

I worried at first that I would regret it or feel upset. But an amazing experience happened. I suddenly felt like my soul had be awoken once more... I felt light, free, alive. I felt the happiest I had done in ages.

I felt like I had come full circle, only there was a change. The witch the dreads brought out stayed, even when the dreads got cut out. Sometimes you don't appreciate what you already had in the first place. I don't regret my dread journey at all, and I am a big believer in never say never. I might in time get dreads again, although I think I would grow and dread my real hair.

What I have learned from the experience is that when you have dreads, there is nowhere to hide. Everyone looks at you. Judging, rolling their eyes, something to say on the subject. But I was able to stand in a room full of people and not give a damn what someone thought. The dreads brought out the real witch within me... and through this healing experience I was able to grow and become the most comfortable I have ever felt as a Witch.

Only in my pain, did I find my will. Only in the chaos, did I learn to be still. Only in the fear, did I find my might. Only in my darkness, did I see my light -
(T.M.T)

FORGETFUL MAGICK

One thing I have noticed as I become older is my memory from time to time tries to deceive or trick me. I think this may have something to do with working for spirit. Often after a reading I cannot remember what we have talked about or discussed. It's as if I go into a bit of a haze, day dream or another world.

Often later that day I will feel a little bit dopey or forgetful. This then causes me to forget where I may have left a set of keys, or other objects. If you suffer with the same level of witchy scattiness, here are a couple of quick easy spells that may help you:

Forgetful Magick Spell - Find A Lost Object

To perform this spell, you will need the power of your intention.

Say in thought or out loud:

Keeper Of What Disappears

Hear Me Now...Open Your Ears

Find For Me What I Now Seek

By Moon, Sun, Earth, Air, Fire & Sea

This Is My Will. It's Done So Mote It Be.

Forgetful Magick Spell - Return A Lost Item

To perform this spell, you will need the power of your intention.

Say in thought or out loud:

What I've Lost
Help Me To Find
So I May Restore
My Piece Of Mind
Bring It To Sight
Bring It This Night
As I Will It
So Mote It Be!

Forgetful Magick Spell - Locate A Lost Object

To perform this spell, you will need a purple or grey candle and the power of your intention.

Light a purple or grey candle and stare into the flame. Say in thought or out loud:

Object I Seek
Come To Me
Wherever Ye Hide
I Shall See
And As My Work So Mote It Be

Continue to stare into the flame, visualising the lost object being found.

Forgetful Magick Spell - Return Spell

To perform this spell, you will need the power of your intention.

Say in thought or out loud:

Take Us Back From

Whence We Came

To Time And Place

That Are The Same

Let Past Be Present

That Time Regain

Forgetful Magick Spell - Forget A Memory

To perform this spell, you will need the power of your intention.

Say in thought or out loud:

Thoughts

Beliefs

Ideas

Truths

Images

All Of These You Hold On To Tightly

What I Now Mention

You Will Release, And Welcome In An Inner Peace

Forgetfulness of your real nature is true death; remembrance of it is rebirth - Ramana Maharshi

BLESSINGS MAGICK

From time to time we are all blessed with the new energy that comes into our world. This maybe in the form of celebrating the life we have and the love around us. It may be in the form of a new home, a new job, a new life into the world, or something else new which allows us to write a new chapter in our personal book of life. The demands put upon us by the physical world, can sometimes stops us from remembering and celebrating that life in all forms is a gift. I wanted to share with you a couple of blessing spells that I have done that are, simple but powerful. Try and enjoy the beauty of your world.

Blessings Magick Spell - The Gift Of Life

To perform this spell, you will need the power of your intention.

Say in thought or out loud:

Sacred Mother Of All That Is

I Revel In Thy Divine Bliss

You Walk With Me In Thy Shining Light

Throughout The Day And The Night

You Surround & Enfold Me With Your Loving Care

You Are My Rock, My Foundation, You Are Always There

Great Mother Goddess Gives The Breath Of Life

Hold Me Safe From Harm & Safe From Strife

May I Forever Walk In Thy Blessed Light

May It Dwell Within Me, May It Shine So Bright

In Thy Perfect love & Harmony
In Thy Perfect Trust... So Mote It Be!

Blessings Magick Spell - Home Blessings

To perform this spell, you will need the power of your intention.

Say in thought or out loud:

Smoke Of Air
And Fire Of Earth
Cleanse And Bless
This Home And Hearth
Drive Away
All Harm And Fear
Only Good
May Enter Here

Blessings Magick Spell - Witches Blessings

To perform this spell, you will need to cast it under a full Moon and use the power of your intention.

Say in thought or out loud:

I Call To The Witches
Both Near And Far
No Need To Name You
You Know Who You Are

Come Dance With Me

By The Fire Light

And Give Praise To The Goddess

This Full Moon Night

It Doesn't Matter Where You Are

Send Your Soul

It Travels Far

I'll Wait For You

As The Sun Goes To Rest

Tonight I Will Be Truly Blessed

Brothers Sisters Dance With Me

As I Will It

So Mote It Be

Blessings Magick Spell - Child Blessings

To perform this spell, you will need a coloured candle of choice that represents your child, an athame, a photo of your child and the power of your intention.

Choose a candle that most represents your child. The colour of the candle greatly influences the type of energy released by the flame.

With your athame, carve the child's name into the candle. Place a photo of the child underneath the candle and spend some time thinking of the feelings you have for them. Light the candle.

Then, say in thought or out loud:

Sweet Child Of Mine, Dear (Child's Name)

Whom The Moon Has Kissed

And The Sun Has Graced

May your Health Be In Tip Top Shape

May Your Mind And Wit Burn Bright

May Your Travels Be Without Fright

May You Laugh Often For You Shall See

This Flame Is Magical As Your Inner Light To Me

And May That Light Be Strong And Always Burn Bright

A Beacon To Attract All That Is Just And Right

This Candle Burns With Love, By All The Powers Of

Three Times Three

Witnessed By The Divine, So Shall It Be

Allow the candle to burn out. You may wish to perform this blessing each year or on a special day for instance birth date.

Blessing Magick Spell - New Job Blessings

To perform this spell, you will need the power of your intention.

Say in thought or out loud:

Great Mother Goddess, I Give Thanks to Thee

For Allowing Me Job Security

A Place To Grow, And Flourish Forward

Abundance, Prosperity

I wish I May, I Wish I Might

Be Blessed With All The Magick

You've Given Me Tonight

By The Power In Me

Thank you Goddess Now Blessed Be

Talk about your Blessings more than you talk about your burdens - Author Unknown

LOVE MAGICK

Love... Love is a tricky subject isn't it? I've had to think very carefully about this part of the book, and what to include and what to leave out. For me love spells are some of the most dangerous to perform. You have to be super careful when you dabble with matters of the heart. Through my witchcraft I am a big believer in someone having free will, and this is why I feel you have to be careful with this subject. So many times people have asked me can I perform a spell to make somebody fall in love with a person? I have two problems with this... Firstly by casting a spell of that nature you are forcing your energy onto someone. You are taking away that person's free will! Whilst there are spells out there to do such a thing, for me personally as a witch it's not ethically right, and so I choose to not use my magick in this way.

The second issue I have is if you have to use magick for somebody to find you attractive, desirable, or to love you... they were never good enough to have your heart in the first place. Why would you want to be with someone that you know has only come about from a spell? Whilst it might seem perfect for a time, it's a bit like wearing a mask. It would be an illusion and you would run the risk of the mask slipping, incurring a cost to yourself further down the road. It might be in time the spell became broken - and could result in you having a broken heart. Better to leave this subject for cupid to shoot his arrow.

When you do experience the true power of real love, this is some of the most powerful magick you will ever come across. But it can't be forced or obtained because you feel you are owed it, or you feel time is running out for you. Love... like many things happens when the time is right. Often when we are least looking for it, that's when the magick finds us.

I've also had situations before where somebody may have fallen in love with the wrong person... a married person, or they may have fallen in love with someone who is gay or sexually not compatible for their needs, and they want to change that energy. Sadly, again this is not ethical practice and you are blocking or stopping that person from being them self.

Remember like everything, if you misuse magick it can backfire, and come at a cost to yourself. Always keep your intentions pure for the highest of good.

What you can do with love magick however... is try to make the road a-head a little easier for new love to find you. Here are some types of spells that could be used and don't interfere with anybody's free will...

Sometimes when people seek love spell guidance it could be, they may have become caught up in a love triangle situation. If that's the case and you are unsure of what way to jump this spell is perfect at restoring mind-set and bringing balance to the situation...

Love Magick Spell - Clarity

To perform this spell, you will need a yellow or white candle and the power of your intention.

Light a yellow or white candle, send your thoughts that you would like clarity on into the flame, and then say in thought or out loud:

See The Candle Burning Bright

Let My Mind See The Light

Take The Fog Far Away

So I Can Cleary See The Way

Give Me Clarity And Light

So I Can Focus Through The Night

Love Magick Spell - Manifest True Love

To perform this spell, you will need the power of your intention.

Think of all the positive qualities you would want from a new partner. Spend time creating or manifesting this vision within your third eye. Then say in thought or out loud:

To Find True Love...

I Conjure Thee

I Conjure Thee

I'm The Queen

You're The Bee

As I Desire, So Shall It Be

Love Magick Spell - Perfume Spell Attract the Love Of Your Life

To perform this spell, you will need your favourite perfume or after shave, a pink candle, athame, to be performed on a full Moon and the power of your intention.

Carve a heart into the pink candle with your athame and then light it. Place the candle either outside in the light of the full moon, or in a window which receives moonlight. The perfume or aftershave bottle should sit on the left hand side of the candle. Say in thought or out loud:

Venus, Grant Me The Love That I Lack

Through This Scent

My Mate I Attract

Allow the candle to burn out. Wear the fragrance each time you go out and about. It will draw a new love toward you.

Love Magick Spell - To Bring True Love

To perform this spell, you will need the power of your intention.

Say in thought or out loud:

Goddess, Moon, And Stars Above

Let My Life Be Blessed With Love

I Call upon The Fertile Earth

Send To Me A Heart Of Worth

I Call upon The Sacred Water

Grant This Wish Unto Thy Daughter

I Call Upon The Swirling Air

May I Be Held In Tender Care

I Call Upon The Steadfast Stone

Never More To Be Alone

I Call Upon The Burning Fire

Bind Me True To My Desire

Earth, Water, Air And Stone

Fire, Blood, Flesh & Bone

Goddess, Moon, And Stars Above

Let My Life Be Blessed With Love

Love Magick Spell - *Self Love For True Love*

To perform this spell, you will need the power of your intention.

Say in thought or out loud:

I Understand My Heart Is Key

And True love Starts

With Love For Me

I Attract The Love

I Feel I Deserve

So I Seek Connection

I Can Forever Preserve

Love Magick Spell - *Soul Mate*

To perform this spell, you will need the power of your intention.

Say three times in thought or out loud:

Bring Henceforth To Me

A Soul Mate

Loving And True

A Perfect Match

For All To See

A Twin Flame

Out Of The Blue

So Mote It Be!

*Maybe it's true, maybe we don't know what we have until we've lost it. But, maybe it's also true that we don't know what we're missing until we find it -
Author Unknown*

FERTILITY MAGICK

Whilst I don't have or don't intend on ever having children of my own, only my fur baby children! I am blessed to know of a few children that have come into this world through the gift of magick. Children that are conceived by magick are very special souls indeed. Often, they are young witchlings with the purest of hearts, and they see the beauty in the world around them. They have a rare gift, which is the ability to light up a room and fill it with love and laughter. These are children of the Earth, often old souls, with deep knowledge and wisdom. They come into this world with the gift of being able to heal, all whom come into their presence.

Fertility magick is a powerful thing. I have seen it touch the lives of friends and clients, who would have never been able to have children under normal circumstances. Magick is a demanding mistress and she will decide ultimately, if the circumstances are right for a child to be gifted and come into this world.

Before you seek the powers of fertility magick, always look at the physical world around you. One thing I have seen time and time again through my readings with clients, is that sometimes people are desperately wanting a child but for the wrong reasons. Sometimes it could be a relationship is going through a rocky patch, and they feel that a child is the answer to save that relationship. I've also seen people trying to reclaim part of their youth, and how when they had their first child they felt so happy. These people are wanting a child for the wrong reasons. Whilst I am sure they would love a child that came into their world, if you want a child to fix a problem, - you are not ready to call upon the powers of fertility magick. It's no good thinking a child will solve everything. The cracks will still remain underneath the surface, and at some stage you will have to answer to that energy. You also run the risk of that child becoming damaged in the future. Especially if a relationship should end badly or break down.

So, before you seek fertility magick look at the physical world around you. Are you in a stable relationship… where you love your partner unconditionally? Have you or your partner got a stable income… to support a new life within this world? Have you got a stable home… where you can comfortably bring a child into? The more you can say yes to these questions, the more you are ready to work with fertility magick, and the greater the chances are of the spell working for the highest of good. Ultimately, can you give that child the unconditional love it deserves regardless of sex, how it looks, or any elements it may have coming into this world? If you can answer yes with truth in your heart, you can look at performing the below spells…

Fertility Magick Spell - Partnership Spell

To perform this spell, you will need nine white candles, yourself and your partner and the power of your intention.

Before having intercourse or at your most fertile time. Light the nine candles in a circle around you and your partner, and then say this spell together before consummating, in thought or out loud:

With One Mind, We Call To Thee

With One Heart, We Long For Thee

Child Of Earth, Wind, Fire & Sea

Into Our Lives, We Welcome Thee

Fertility Magick Spell - Enchanted Egg

To perform this spell, you will need two fresh eggs, a brown paper bag, a piece of cotton or twine, to be performed on a Waning Moon, and the power of your intention.

On the night of a waning Moon, place two fresh eggs in a small brown paper bag and seal the bag with a piece of cotton or twine. Say in thought or out loud:

Eggs To Earth As Moon Mourns Dust

A Bag Of Two, A Pack Of Lust

Mother Earth Shall Hold Them Warm

And On My Union Place Her Charm

Bury the bag before the Sun rises, in a secret place. Take care not to break the eggs.

Fertility Magick Spell - Pregnancy

To perform this spell, you will need the power of your intention.

Say in thought three times, or out loud:

It Is Time Of Harvest

Your Womb Fills

The Ears Of The Grain Are Swollen

Your Womb Fills

The Ears Of The Grain Are Splitting

It Is Time

Bring Fourth!

Bring Fourth!

Bring Fourth!

In The Power & The Love

Fertility Magick Spell - New Life

To perform this spell with your partner you will need the power of your intention.

Say in thought or out loud:

Mother And Father Of All Growing Things

Unto My Being Your Golden Love Bring

Bless This Seed To Fulfil It's Design

Of Leaf And Fruit, Of Blossom And Vine

With One Mind, We Call To Thee

With One Heart, We Long For Thee

Child Of Earth, Wind, Fire & Sea
Into Our Lives, We Welcome Thee

*Let your hopes, not your hurts, shape your future -
Robert H. Schuller*

FRUITFUL MAGICK

You are maybe learning by now just how many weird and wonderful ways magick can be used in our everyday world. Another easy way to work with magick is through the use of fruit. Often as a family we have an array of fruits in our bowl every week. How often do you throw old fruit away? Now you can use it within spell work... I am also blessed to have certain fruit trees and bushes within my own garden. These are perfect for spell work as when the time is right, mother nature releases her treasures allowing me to put them to good use. Often not in cooking but in the power of magick...

Below are some fun spells you can try with various fruits...

Magical tip - Use lemon juice to write sigils and protection symbols everywhere. Doorposts, doors, walls, cabinets, books, book pages, work desks... The ink is invisible, so the possibilities are endless. What's more, lemon juice is generally safe on most surfaces (aside from brass-plated items, which it damages) and smells nice too. Lemons are associated with cleansing and purification, which can add an extra little boost to your sigils and protection symbols.

Fruitful Magick Spell - Orange Upliftment

To perform this spell, you will need an orange, be near running water and the power of your intention.

Use of oranges in spells injects warmth, stimulates the senses and brings optimism. In this spell the orange invokes the power of the Sun to create happiness.

At noon go to a place near a river, lake or sea. Hold your orange in your left hand and start to peel the skin. With each piece of skin you peel make a wish for happiness, and say in thought or out loud:

By The Power Of The Sun

My Spell Is Done

May The Brightness Illuminate

The Darkest Depths

Then throw your orange as high as you can towards the Sun, and let it land within the water

Magical tip - Pour cinnamon tea on the front step of your business, to bring in customers and their money

Fruitful Magick Spell - The Bombshell Potion

To perform this spell, you will need 1 tbsp of raw unfiltered apple cider vinegar, 1/2 cup fresh pineapple juice, 1 tbsp of fresh lime juice, 1 tbsp of honey and the power of your intention.

Mix ingredients well and say in thought or out loud:

Magick Potion, Make Me Well

Bring Balance To Body

Cast My Spell

So Mote It Be

Then drink the potion. Pineapple juice is said to have anti-inflammatory properties, aid in digestion, help with kidney health and packed with vitamins and antioxidants. With lots of B vitamins, pineapple is a natural energy booster. Raw apple cider vinegar has high levels of potassium and calcium. It's said to help with digestion, detoxification and may help regulate blood pressure and cholesterol.

Magical tip - Cut an apple into half across it's middle, instead of from top to bottom as you normally wood. When you open an apple, a pentacle is revealed.

Fruitful Magick Spell - Apple Blessings

To perform this spell, you will need an apple, lemon, herbs (marigold, thyme, basil, yarrow, a Cauldron, water, salt, besom/broom and the power of your intention.

Cut half a lemon and apple. Keep two pieces either side of your cauldron and put the other two halves inside the cauldron. Say in thought or out loud:

In This Pot I Stir The Sun

And Follow The Rule Of Harming None

Banishment Of Bane When

Going Widdershins

And With Water And Salt Negativity Is Cleansed (Throw these in the cauldron)

Household Duties Are More Than Chores

Magick Abounds When Mopping Floors

With This Broom I Do Sweep (Sweep With Broom)

To Cleanse My House And Safely Keep

Marigold, Basil, Thyme & Yarrow (Throw into cauldron)

My Spell Is Cast For a Better Tomorrow

Lemons For Joy & Apples For Health

The Power Within Brings Great Wealth

And In This Kitchen I Do Pray

To Truly Walk the Witches Way

These are just some ways you can work with fruit. There are many others so have fun and see what you feel drawn to working with... here are some other basic fruits and their magical meanings...

Apple - known as the Fruit of the Gods, is a very powerful source of spiritual energy that encourages balance and harmony. The Wiccan Feast of Apples is celebrated on Samhain (Halloween), and in ancient Greece and Rome, apples were eaten at Diana's Festival (August 13). If cut horizontally, the apple reveals the pentagram pattern, which is considered the gateway to occult powers as well as symbol of the quintessence. The Egyptians offered apples to their highest and most powerful priests, whom they considered guardians of hidden knowledge. In the Middle Ages, sliced apples were used to foretell the future and eating them regularly was said to enable a person to live over 200 years. Modern clinical studies have proved that eating apples reduces cancer risk. Air - element

Apricots - have been grown on the mountainous slopes of China for over 5,000 years, though the fruit is much more difficult to grow in temperate regions. Apricots carry feminine spiritual energy and are used to sweeten someone's disposition or instill romance and passion in a relationship. Extremely rich in vitamins and minerals, apricots strengthen the immune system and have more of the antioxidant carotene than any other fruit. Air - element.

Banana - an everyday food that is a fruit and ruled by Mars. Prevents harm and accidents while traveling cross-country or by air. To increase sexual stamina - dry and crush the banana into a powder and then rub it on your body. It has powerful lust properties because of its obvious shape. Air - element

Blackberries - or brambleberries, currants, and raspberries promote wealth and protect from evil. The protective thorniness of their deep-rooted bushes is the plant's alchemical signature. Blackberry pies are baked for the Wiccan celebration of Lughnasadh (August 2) to protect crops and encourage a bountiful harvest, and blackberry tea is said to protect the stomach from disease. Raspberries alleviate watery complaints such as diarrhea and painful menstruation. Earth – element.

Blueberries - embody the esoteric principles of calm acceptance, peace, and a protected environment. For centuries, witches have eaten blueberry tarts when under psychic attack to protect themselves. Earth – element.

Cherries - have long been associated with feminine energy and divination and are used in spells throughout the world to attract suitors and discern the future. The cherry is a cousin of the plum and has been known to mankind since Neolithic times. The fruit is diuretic, easily digested, and it is recommended as an acceptable sugar for diabetics and a cure for gout. Air – element.

Cranberries - provide protective energy and fight off negative influences. In modern rituals, the juice is sometimes substituted for wine. Some evidence suggests the deep red berries prevent bladder infections. Water – element.

Grapefruit - is derived from a bitter citrus fruit known as the pomelo, which was cross-pollinated with the orange to make it sweeter. However, the grapefruit was not recognized as a distinct species of citrus fruit until the nineteenth century. The tangy fruit increases metabolism, which is why it is often eaten after breakfast and used for bodily detoxification. Fire – element.

Grapes - carry spiritual energy and increase mental fertility, opening us to meaningful dreams and visions. Eating grapes or raisins is said to increase a woman's fertility. See Wine. Air – element.

Kiwi - is the small, dark-brown fruit of a subtropical vine. The hairy, egg-shaped fruit has a green pulp with a tart strawberry flavour. Kiwis are considered by some native cultures to be plant testicles, and like strawberries, are eaten to encourage physical love and zesty romance. Earth – element.

Lemons - are another citrus fruit that did not become widely known until the Middle Ages. They soon became very popular and were thought to encourage longevity and faithfulness. Lemon pie fortifies fidelity, and lemon slices on a stranger's plate or under his chair guarantees his or her friendship. Lemon juice is a powerful cleaning agent and is used to wash magical implements of all types of toxicity. A cleansing tea is made from dried lemon peels. Fire – element.

Lime - cleanses the palate and refreshes the soul. It is used in purification and healing rituals. Fire – element.

Mango - is sacred to Buddha, and it is considered one of the most spiritually charged and elevating fruits. Air – element.

Melons - come from the same family of vines that includes squash and cucumbers. The first wild melons were extremely bitter, and it has taken millennia of selective cultivation to produce the sweet varieties we know today. In the Middle Ages, melons were still viewed with suspicion; it was believed that eating them would make you more vulnerable to the plague and other epidemics. During the Renaissance, the cantaloupe was developed at special monasteries for consumption only by the popes, and melons gradually became more fashionable in Europe. Watermelon is the oldest edible melon and was sacred to the Egyptian god of chaos, Set. Water – element.

Oranges - this fruit is well known all over the world and dates back to prehistory. Can be used in love, joy, and inspiration magic. Placed in stockings on Christmas as sympathetic magic to encourage the return of the sun. Directly associated to the sun and solar magick. Eat to lift your spirits. Dry and grind into a powder to use in love and abundance spells. Fire – element.

Peaches - are a feminine symbol of love, spiritual fertility, and wishes come true. Serving peach pie to someone helps win his or her love and attention. In Asia, the peach is a symbol of virginity, and the blossoming of the peach tree is a sign of spring and youthful purity. Magic wands made of peach wood are used in exorcisms. Air – element.

Pears - initiate lustful passion by stimulating the Sacral Chakra, and the fruit is associated with Venus, the goddess of love. In the Middle Ages, it was believed eating a pear would immediately induce sexual arousal. Surprisingly, pears were unknown in most ancient cultures, and it was not until the Romans that they were cultivated. Air – element.

Pineapple - was brought from the New World to Europe in the sixteenth century and was thought to resemble an oversize pinecone, hence the name. Pineapple juice is drunk to ensure chastity; eating the fruit brings luck and prosperity. For those reasons, pineapples are traditionally used in spells for the protection of a person's possessions, including one's spouse and children. Pineapples are known to contain a very powerful digestive enzyme and are part of many popular weight-loss diets. Fire – element.

Plums - and prunes are said to inspire constant love when served to someone you desire. The Dakota Indians stuck wild plum stalks into the ground to attract favourable attention from the Great Spirit, and the Egyptians and Greeks considered plums relaxing to both mind and body. Air – element.

Pomegranate - is sacred to Persephone and Ceres, gods of growth and fertility. Pagans regarded the fruit as a symbolic womb, and the red juice of the pomegranate is used as ink in modern magical rituals. Eating a pomegranate with a desire strong in mind is considered a magical act that will grant your wish. Earth – element.

Raspberries - induce stamina and vigor, and at one time, the leaves were carried by pregnant women to help them through childbirth. The tea acts as a blood tonic to treat anemia and stop diarrhea. Earth – element.

Strawberries - were not cultivated until the 1600s and soon became a sensation in Europe. They were usually dipped in wine before eaten, and strawberries in cream were originally reserved for women and children only. French King Louis XIV became addicted to strawberries, and even though his doctors forbade him, he continued to indulge his taste for the delectable fruit. The king even sponsored a competition for the best poetry about the strawberry. Strawberries are sacred to the Scandinavian fertility god, Freyr, and are served to promote physical love and zesty romance. Strawberry leaves are placed on serving plates or carried for good luck. The dried leaves make a mildly laxative tea. The word "strawberry" refers to the bed of straw packed around the plants to protect the berries from touching the dirt. Earth – element.

Vegetable Magick

You don't have to just limit yourself to fruit... Vegetables can also be used in many weird and wonderful spells and potions...

Asparagus - was one of the few vegetables introduced into the New World by colonists from Europe, where its use dated back to the days of the Roman Empire. The phallic-shaped plant has always had a reputation as a potent aphrodisiac, which was one of the primary reasons people ate it. The strong odour produced in the urine after asparagus is eaten betrayed many unfaithful husbands who believed in the vegetable's licentious powers. In the Victorian era, mothers made a point of teaching their daughters how to recognize its distinctive smell. Asparagus is also a diuretic and eases stomach and intestinal disorders. Water – element.

Broccoli - is a type of cabbage grown for its flower heads. It is sacred to the god Jupiter, and the Romans believed it increased physical strength and leadership qualities. A chemical in the vegetable is known to retard cancerous growths in the body. Water – element.

Brussel sprouts - are a type of cabbage cultivated since the 1600s for their ball-shaped buds. The vegetable is said to encourage the qualities of stability and endurance. Water – element.

Cabbage - is one of the oldest vegetables known to man, and the alchemists considered it the First Matter of foods. Today, there are over 400 varieties growing all over the world. Green or red "head" cabbage is popular in the West, while the broad-leafed varieties are popular in Asia. Esoterically, cabbage has a strong lunar presence and allows one to tap into existing bodily energies by stimulating the Base Chakra. In fact, several Greek philosophers claimed to live to a very advanced age by eating only cabbages. In Medieval Europe, good neighbors brought newlyweds some cabbage soup on the first morning after they were married, and cabbage was the first thing planted in their gardens to ensure that their love took root. The fertilizing powers of cabbage were considered so powerful in France, that a whole folklore grew up around rumours of spontaneous "cabbage patch babies" that appeared from nowhere. Water – element.

Carrots - carry masculine energy that is said to increase fertility and dispel illusions. Fire – element.

Cauliflower - is a variety of cabbage plant cultivated for its distinctive bouquet shape. The vegetable became popular in ancient Greece, where it was eaten to release feminine energies and initiate lunar cycles. Collard greens are the outside leaves of cauliflower and are used in salads or steamed and eaten hot. Water – element.

Celery stalks - are used to ground unspoken passions and induce lust. While the seeds aid in concentration and produce mental clarity, they have a simultaneous calming effect on the body and are known to lower blood pressure. Air – element.

Cucumber - promotes chastity and hinders lustful behaviour. Conversely, if the dried seeds are consumed by a woman, it increases her fertility. Cucumber peels are said to diminish headaches if placed on the forehead and relieve the pain of arthritis when wrapped around inflamed joints. Water – element.

Garlic - was known and used at least as far back as 3000 BC. In early antiquity, it was sacred to the goddess Hecate and left at crossroads as a sacrifice to her. The pungent cloves were also used for protection against evil and to break curses and hexes, and psychic cooks rub garlic into pots and pans to remove negative influences that might contaminate food. When eaten, garlic stimulates the immune system to protect the body, although it is said to induce lustful behaviour in some people. Garlic is a proven antibiotic, cholesterol reducer, blood pressure reducer, and general heart remedy. Fire – element.

Leeks - are related to onions and are used to drive away evil and impurity. People who eat leeks at the same table are said to form a lifelong bond. Fire – element.

Lettuce - was sacred to the Egyptian fertility god Min, because the local variety was phallic-shaped and oozed a milky secretion. In most other cultures, lettuce is associated with female or lunar goddesses. Esoterically, lettuce invokes feminine energies for protection and psychic centering. It was called Sleep Wort in the Middle Ages, because people believed it enabled them to sleep better. Iceberg lettuce is a head lettuce, while romaine and red varieties are leafy and carry more Air Element. Water – element.

Mushrooms - have been described as vegetable flesh, and like animal flesh, they are eaten to acquire strength and courage. Clinical studies show they boost the immune system and have anti-viral and anti-tumor properties. Because they appear overnight or grow from putrefying organic matter, mushrooms have many superstitions associated with them, and few ancient cultures admitted to eating them. In fact, the mushroom is one of the few foods not mentioned in the Bible. Moreover, many mushroom species are poisonous or produce psychedelic effects that were used by shamans and priests who wanted to keep them secret. Earth – element.

Onions - were worshipped in ancient Egypt for their ability to absorb impurities, and the Egyptians even swore to onions when they took oaths. American colonists hung onions over doorways to protect their families from infectious diseases, and onions are still used in exorcism rituals. Esoterically, onions stand for both physical and spiritual health and protection. Scallions and shallots are green onions with long stems and bulbous roots. Leeks are also a kind of onion. Fire – element.

Potatoes - are a very recent addition to mankind's menu. The tubers are members of the deadly nightshade family, and for centuries, they were thought to be poisonous, cause leprosy, and carry other infectious diseases. It was actually against the law to grow potatoes in France, and the Germans used them only as animal feed. But in the late 1760s, church and government leaders began to promote the potato as a solution to the devastating famine caused by the Seven Years War. Before long, potatoes were a staple of the Western diet. Today, there are over 3,000 varieties, including such unexpected family members as the purple-skinned eggplant. Potatoes are powerful reservoirs of primal energy, and poppets (little dolls) are still fashioned from potatoes as a focus for materialization magic. However, they are still viewed with suspicion by many psychics. The "sleeping prophet" Edgar Cayce warned people to eat only the skins of potatoes and throw away the white pulp. Earth – element.

Radish - protects from the Evil Eye. It turns into sexual energy when eaten and stimulates the Sacral Chakra. Fire – element.

Rhubarb - increases willpower and reduces worry. Rhubarb pie served to a lover places him or her under your power. Chard is rhubarb leaf, which is used sparingly in salads. Rhubarb is also known to alleviate stomach problems. Earth – element.

Sprouts - bring a vitalizing energy to salads and sandwiches. Used fresh, they add both nutritional and esoteric essences to foods. Alfalfa seed and beans such as lentils, soy, garbanzo, mung, and aduki are the best tasting sprouts. Air – element.

Sweet Potatoes - are the tubers of a climbing plant that grows in the southern United States. Yams are the club-shaped rhizomes of an entirely different plant that grows in the West Indies. Both foods look and taste similar and represent gentle nurturing that adds a softening influence to meat dishes. Earth – element.

Tomatoes - were called Love Apples when they were first introduced into Europe from the New World and were used to solicit romantic attention. Europeans also placed them on windowsills to repel negative energies. It seems that nobody thought of cooking with tomatoes until the nineteenth century, and today, the once lowly tomato is the basic ingredient of many sauces, soups, and salads worldwide. Water – element.

Turnips - are used to ward off unwanted presences. In Europe, carved-out turnips with a burning candle inside were used to scare off evil spirits on Halloween. Similarly, serving someone turnips will cause them to leave you alone. Parsnips taste similar to turnips, though they have a more slender bulb. Kohlrabi is a type of turnip that grows above ground. Rutabagas are also related to turnips. Earth – element.

Watercress - grows wild in the beds of streams and was a favorite vegetable of the Greeks and Romans. It is a pungent plant widely regarded as a carrier of feminine power. In the Middle Ages, watercress was made into a soothing skin ointment. Used in salads or made into a tea, the dark green, shiny leaves are high in vitamin C. Water – element.

One of the secrets of a fruitful life is to forgive everybody, everything, before you go to bed - Ann Landers

CANDLE MAGICK

Candle Magick... is another favourite way of mine to spell cast. There is something very powerful when working with a candle. The beauty of sending your intentions into the flame. There are endless possibilities and ways you can introduce candles within your spell work. Some people like to work with coloured spell candles... the different colours represent different qualities you are maybe needing to use to enhance a spell.

Some people use oils blends to anoint their candles, to amplify the spell. I have done this before. Although for me I find this process a little long winded. I tend to only use that if I need to call upon a hardcore spell. You can also use herbs and spices, to anoint your candles giving them an extra kick to your magick.

You can also keep things really simple and use a good old quick and easy tea-light...

Below is a quick reference list to help you understand, what different colours represent. This will help you when bringing colour into your magick...

Coloured Candle Meanings

White - Destruction of negative energy, peace, truth and purity.

Purple - Spiritual awareness, wisdom, tranquility.

Lavender - Intuition, paranormal, peace, healing.

Blue and Deep Blue - Meditation, healing, forgiveness, inspiration, fidelity, happiness, and opening lines of communication.

Green - Money, fertility, luck, abundance, health (not to be used when diagnosed with Cancer), success.

Rose and Pink - Positive self-love, friendship, harmony, joy.

Yellow - Realising and manifesting thoughts, confidence, bringing plans into action, creativity, intelligence, mental clarity, clairvoyance.

Orange - Joy, energy, education, strength attraction, stimulation.

Red - Passion, energy, love, lust, relationships, sex, vitality, courage.

Black - Protection, absorption and destruction of negative energy, also repelling negative energy from others.

Silver - Goddess or feminine energy, remove negativity, psychic development.

Gold - Male energy, Solar energy, fortune, spiritual attainment.

If you're crafty you can also have a go at making your own candles. Some people like to include herbs and oil blends to make them smell nice when burning.

Magick Tip - Never blow out a candle in works of magick. It is said that if you do, you blow away the spirits you work with. Instead use a candle snuffer or you can wet your thumb and forefinger and pinch the wick quickly.

Below are some spells I have used with the power of the flame - This area of magick has so many avenues and there are many books on candle magick alone. As with everything we have looked at so far you will find what does and doesn't work for, you may also enjoy writing your own spells.

Candle Magick Spell - Radiant Health

To perform this spell, you will need a black candle, sage incense and the power of your intention.

Burn a black candle with a sage incense stick, cone, or loose blend next to the candle. Concentrate on removing any health problems, or recent illness you may have had. Say in thought or out loud:

As This Candle Burns

So The Illness Turns

Melted Like This Wax

Cut Like With An Axe

All Disabilities Vanished

As My Word You See

Radiant Health Blessed Be

Let the candle burn right out. Then bury the candle stub and incense ashes, far away from your home. This spell can be performed once per week, until health has improved. This has helped me before when I've been run down or had winter or summer bugs.

Candle Magick Spell - Witches Good Luck

To perform this spell, you will need an orange candle, and the power of your intention.

At midnight, light an orange candle, and say in thought or out loud:

Brimstone, Moon & Witches Fire

Candlelight's Bright Spell

Good Luck I Shall Acquire

Work Thy Magic Well

Midnight Twelve, The Witching Hour

Bring The Luck I Seek

By Wax & Wick Now Work The Power

As These Words I Speak

Harming None, This Spell Is Done

By Law Of Three So Mote It Be

Leave the candle to burn right out.

Candle Magick Spell - Call To Action

To perform this spell, you will need a white candle and the power of your intention.

Say in thought or out loud:

Humbly I Call To Thee

Great Cosmic Energy

Come To My Side & Be My Guide

With All The Richness You Provide

I Will Keep My Head Up & My Heart Open

As My Desires To You Are Spoken

I Call To Thee Profound Energy

Fill Me With Winning Motivation & Strategy

Come To My Side & Be My Guide

I Call To Thee Cosmic Energy

Focus on sending your desires into the flame. Spend some time meditating and watching the flame. Allow the candle to burn out

Candle Magick Spell - *To Find New Employment*

To perform this spell, you will need a yellow or gold candle and the power of your intention.

Begin on a Sunday, light the yellow or gold candle then say in thought or out loud:

A Good Job Awaits Me

For Thy Brilliant Light Scans & Searches

A Place For Me

A Good Job Awaits Me

For Thy Goodness Is Great

My Faith In Thee Is Complete

A Good Job Waits For Me

Repeat this three times. Perform this spell daily until employment is found.

Candle Magick Spell - *Home Protection*

To perform this spell, you will need two black or two white candles and the power of your intention.

Light two black or white candles either side of your front door. Say in thought or out loud:

Bless This House

May Peace Dwell Within

Protect All That Enter

Whether Friend Or Kin

Bless Every Door, Window, Ceiling & Wall

Bless Each Room, Closet, Basement, Bless It All

Bless The Roof & Ground Surrounding With Your

Protective Love & Light

Hold Us In Your Loving Care

Every Second Of Every Day & Night

As Above And So Below

So Mote It Be

Allow the candles to fully burn out.

Thousands of candles can be lighted from a single candle, and the life of that candle will not be shortened. Happiness never decreases by being shared - Author Unknown

CRYSTAL MAGICK

One of my guilty pleasures has to be crystals... Whether it's in a crystal shop, or psychic fayre or witches market, I struggle to walk past without being able to have a look and see what goodies await. I have crystals everywhere in every room around my home, within my garden, and also at the front of my house. Crystals like anything else are a powerful tool when used in spell work.

Here is a little break-down of some of the 20 most popular crystals and their healing and magical uses.

1. Selenite: The Master

This master mineral is one of the only healing crystals that does not need to be charged and can actually be used to cleanse and recharge other crystals. It is the most abundant crystal - and is found in ancient evaporated salt lakes and seas and can be found from Mexico to Brazil and beyond.

Metaphysical healing properties: Selenite is a conduit to the highest level of conscious and all that is infinite – spirit guides, the universe, and intuition. It brings the spirit world to earth and reminds us where we come from, and where we are going after this life.

Physical healing properties: Known for its master healing properties, there isn't much that selenite can't be used for. Meditating on a desired outcome and carrying the stone with you can help to bring great healing and inner peace.

2. Moonstone: The Stabiliser

Deeply linked to the feminine and the moon, moonstone is a perfect stone to gracefully create harmony within and strengthen intuition. It was the stone of Gods and Goddesses in ancient India, and is seen as sacred and regal.

Metaphysical healing properties: Moonstone can open you up to other worlds and the universe at large. It can also be used to combat materialism and manage the ego.

Physical healing properties: Moonstone can be used to aid the pituitary gland and digestive system, obesity, water retention, hormonal problems, menstrual problems.

3. Aventurine: The Stone of Opportunity

Known for amplifying luck, prosperity and abundance, aventurine is a good stone to take with you if you're planning to gamble in Las Vegas. A variety of quartz, this stone attracts luck and assists in the successful application of new opportunities.

Metaphysical healing properties: Associated with the Heart Chakra, aventurine can create a sense of general well-being and emotional calm. It harmonizes the mental, physical and emotional bodies and re-establishes balance.

Physical healing properties: Aventurine is supportive of the heart, blood, and energy circulation, and can help speed up recovery time from an injury, illness, or surgery.

4. Crystal Quartz: The Spirit Stone

Likely the most commonly known crystal, crystal quartz is seen as the window of light into the metaphysical world.

Metaphysical healing properties: This particular crystal contains the entire colour spectrum, and can be used to amplify desires, prayers, and manifestations from the spirit world to the physical world. Meditate with crystal quartz and "programme" the crystal with your intentions. You can then wear or carry your crystal with you to raise your vibration and increase the manifestations of your desires.

Physical healing properties: Crystal quartz is a master healer and is thought to stimulate the immune and circulatory systems - and increase the flow of energy in the body.

5. Citrine: The Money Stone

A type of quartz, the golden, yellow hue of this crystal is associated with its connection to money, gold, and wealth.

Metaphysical healing properties: Carry this stone with you to the bank, to business meetings involving finances, or place citrine on your desk and gaze at it while you work. Citrine can help you attract abundance and financial wealth and stability.

Physical healing properties: Citrine is known to stimulate the metabolism, and aid in digestion and nausea. It can also be used to strengthen nerve impulses, helping the brain fire more rapidly and sharply.

6. Agate: Stone of Inner Stability

This varied stone can be found in nearly all colours with seemingly endless types of striations. From clear transparent, to coloured and wildly banded, agate embodies our inner world and all its states.

Metaphysical healing properties: Agate raises self-awareness, stabilizes the aura (in all its colours), transforms negative energy, and is a powerful conduit of spirit. Use this stone to heal anger, emotional instability, and lack of self worth.

Physical healing properties: Known to improve mental function by improving clarity of thought, agate is a wonderful stone to use before an important test, when writing, or when gathering thoughts for a meaningful conversation with someone you love and wish to communicate clearly with.

7. Tourmaline: The Grounding Stone

The preferred talisman of protection, tourmaline is used as a psychic shield to ground your energy and combat the entry of negative entities in your energy field. Long used by wizards, shamans, witches and magicians, tourmaline can be found on every continent.

Metaphysical healing properties: Although tourmaline is black as night, it can be used to ward off negative energies, raise your vibration, and usher you into the light. Black absorbs light, as this stone acts as a sponge for harmful or dark energies. It encourages you to remain radiant during dark times.

Physical healing properties: Use tourmaline to ease pain in the joints and to assist in realigning the spine. It can also be used to strengthen the immune system, heart and adrenal glands – easing stress and releasing tension.

8. Rose Quartz: The Love Stone

This beautiful pink quartz is associated with the heart and expressing unconditional love to self, others, and the planet.

Metaphysical healing properties: A wonderful stone to invite love, assist in giving love and even attract your soul mate, rose quartz is all about the heart. Wear or carry rose quartz to open yourself up to finding love if you're single, and to deepen and nurture your love if you're in a relationship.

Physical healing properties: Centred around the heart chakra, rose quartz can be used for deep emotional healing and release, and has been known to improve circulation and lower blood pressure. It can also be used to ease palpitations or skipped beats, and release tension.

9. Turquoise: The Stone of Protection

Believed to be the oldest stone known to man, turquoise has long been cherished by chiefs, shamans, kings, wizards, and the like. Prized as a symbol of wisdom, turquoise is prevalent in almost all ancient cultures and has always been known as the stone of protection.

Metaphysical healing properties: Turquoise strengthens the meridians in the body and supports intuition and meditation. Because of its blue hue, it is also associated with the Throat Chakra which supports clear communication. Carry turquoise with you as a talisman of protection and to channel the ancient wisdom it emits.

Physical healing properties: Assisting in problems of the brain, neck, ears, and throat, turquoise is very much associated with the psychic realm, making it a great stone to clear blockages and support the healthy flow of energy within the entire body.

10. Fluorite: The Stone of Positivity

This crystal is perhaps one of the most underrated but also one of the most powerful. This stone is known to quite literally suck negative energy and low vibrations from a space or your body, and create room for the light to shine in. Found in multiple colour variations, fluorite is a truly magical crystal.

Metaphysical healing properties: Used for auric protection, to raise your vibration, alchemize negative energy, and calming a chaotic mind. Rainbow fluorite is most known to stabilize the mind and amplify psychic connection and heighten intuitive powers.

Physical healing properties: This dynamic stone can be used when studying to clear the mind and sharpen focus. It can also be used to alleviate inflammation in the body, dissipate cold symptoms, and can be healing for the mucous membrane as well.

11. Lapis Lazuli: The Stone of Truth

This beautiful, blue crystal is one of the most vibrant, ancient, and sought after on earth. It has long been associated with royalty and luxury, and its celestial properties assist those in the physical realm with wisdom and good judgement.

Metaphysical healing properties: Lapis Lazuli activates the ethereal upper chakras and empowers the Throat Chakra for clear communication and ease of expressing one's ideas. This intriguing stone promotes inner observation and truth as it assists in the discovery and representation of the spirit realm.

Physical healing properties: Use this powerful stone to support and help heal the throat, larynx, and vocal cords. Due to its strong ties to the brain, it is believed to ease Attention Deficit Disorder (ADD) by helping the mind to focus and let go of unnecessary thoughts.

12. Hematite: The Grounding Stone

This iron-rich stone is deeply grounding and connected to the earth. It has been referred to as the "bloodstone" in ancient Greece because of the red hue of the iron content when found in nature.

Metaphysical healing properties: Hematite is connected to the Root Chakra and has a profoundly grounding energy that reminds us of our human existence and supports us financially.

Physical healing properties: The iron found in hematite can help us cleanse the blood, improve circulation, manage an irregular menstrual flow, and support a healthy heart. It can also be used to alleviate stress and anxiety and calm the nervous system.

13. Jade: The Dream Stone

This is another dynamic stone that can be found in a multitude of colours all around the world. The region dictates the colour, and this was one of the most widely used stones in ancient times. It has been revered across cultures, continents, and millennia (and into modern day) for its physical and metaphysical healing properties, making it one of the most consistently used crystals known to man.

Metaphysical healing properties: Jade represents nobility of rank and ideals. This stone is also connected to the heart and helps us accept truth, express love (to self and others), and assists in accessing shamanic realms in the dream state.

Physical healing properties: With its association to the heart, Jade is good for filtering toxins and cleansing the body as a whole through the blood. It can also be used to ease joint pain and speed up the healing process after a surgery.

14. Amethyst: The Manifestation Stone

This is one of the most common stones of the New Age, along with selenite and crystal quartz. Amethyst can be found in all corners of the world. This beautiful purple crystal is known for many things, but manifestation is at the top of the list.

Metaphysical healing properties: Connect to your heart's desires and life's purpose with amethyst, and then manifest them in your life! This powerful crystal is associated with the upper chakras, helping us bring the ethereal realm to the physical plane. This includes bringing our earthly dreams to life.

Physical healing properties: Use amethyst to boost the sympathetic nervous system, balance hormones, relieve headaches, ease neck tension, and treating insomnia. Place amethyst under your pillow at night to sleep deeply and wake rested, ready to create and manifest.

15. Kyanite: The Stone of Emotion

Kyanite helps the mind create pathways where none previously existed, especially in terms of emotional development and meditation. It does not accumulate negative energy, so it does not need to be cleansed, and can actually be used to cleanse other stones and spaces. The calming blue-green hue is associated with the sky and therefore is extremely soothing and supportive to the nerves.

Metaphysical healing properties: Psychic abilities can be enhanced with kyanite as it deepens meditation and opens channels to the spirit realm. It can also be used to help those transitioning through death.

Physical healing properties: Kyanite is wonderful to help heal any pain in the throat and improve communication. It can also be used to ease headaches, eye pain from looking at a computer, and tension at the brow.

16. Obsidian: The Mirror Stone

The jet-black stone is the mirror stone for its ability to enhance sight and the way you see the world and circumstances. It's highly reflective surface and consistent colouring allow you to look deeply within to reveal your soul and the healing required to elevate your vibration.

Metaphysical healing properties: Obsidian use dates back to the stone age and its spiritual qualities have been known to allow sight into other worlds, into the soul itself, and into realms not accessible from earth, to gain wisdom and knowledge. Use this stone to reveal your shadow self, flaws, and weaknesses so you can better understand yourself.

Physical healing properties: Use obsidian to relieve emotional distress that has long been buried, ignored, or even wiped from memory. It can also be used to ease stress and anxiety associated with emotional trauma.

17. Blue Topaz: The Stone of Creativity

The bright blue colour of topaz reflects the mind and our potential for creativity. It can help stimulate the mind to learn more quickly and retain information that can be drawn upon for years to come. It is also useful in firing up creativity and opening the mind to new ideas.

-Metaphysical healing properties: As topaz is a stone of the mind, it is great for connecting to one's angels, spirit guides, and passed loved ones. Use topaz to expand the mind, open the soul, and align with the spirit realm.

Physical healing properties: Topaz has long been known to assist with mental illness, diseases of the eyes, dimness in sight, and to restore loss of taste.

18. Opal: The Eye Stone

This brilliant and colourful stone appears to be on fire with a rainbow spectrum of electric colours when moved in the light. It is associated with the eye as it is so pleasing to look at and associated with the Third Eye Chakra. Opal inspires optimism, happiness, appreciation, and a general sense of wellbeing. There are over ten different types of opal, all originating from different parts of the world with slightly different properties.

Metaphysical healing properties: Opal acts as a prism of the entire aura and brings in the entire spectrum of light to the spiritual and energy body. It can amplify a vibrant energy in the soul that is not commonly seen from other stones. Use opal to awaken psychic and mystical qualities, and as a vehicle to connect with ancient spiritual realms.

Physical healing properties: As the stone of the eye, opal can be used to help support the health of eyes and improve vision. It can also stimulate memory and stabilize neurotransmitter disturbances

19. Amazonite: Stone of Courage

Amazonite calms the spirit and soothes the soul with its cool greenish colour. This stone empowers you to seek and express your inner truth with courage and conviction, without being overly emotional.

Metaphysical healing properties: Used to balance and cleanse the chakras, amazonite can soothe emotional trauma stored in the body and help prevent the manifestation of this trauma into a physical illness. It is also useful for harmonizing the relationship between intellect and intuition for a healthy balance that this grounded and enlightened.

Physical healing properties: Typically used for general well-being, amazonite is beneficial to the entire body. Use it more specifically to to soothe rashes, clear acne, and prevent infection to wounds.

20. Garnet: The Stone of Health and Creativity

This highly grounding stone is found the world over in a variety of colours and compositions. It is most known for its qualities of promoting health and the flow of creativity - and bringing spirit down to earth.

Metaphysical healing properties: Garnet helps to remove inhibitions and taboos and allows the mind to think freely and creatively. It invites the spirit to participate in the physical realm and opens the channels of communication and creativity with the inner self for outward expression.

Physical healing properties: Known to stimulate the metabolism, garnet is a wonderful stone to get things in the body moving and, conversely, help clot blood and stop bleeding. It is also used to improve libido and sexual desires.

There are many other beautiful crystals... and I would be able to write a book just on this subject alone. You may already have some favourite crystals that you like to work with. Or like me you are maybe increasing and growing your collection all the time. Like with anything crystals are a very personal thing.

Magick Tip - If you use a clear quartz crystal point. It can be used to scry with. You will in time be able to see spirit guides, spirits and visions or insights. It's said in legend the famous wizard Merlin always carried a clear quartz crystal point for matters of insight, and wisdom.

Here are some crystal spells you may like to try...

Crystal Magick Spell - Calming Spell

To perform this spell, you will need a piece of Amethyst and the power of your intention.

Hold the crystal in your power hand, and say in thought or out loud:

I am Peaceful, I Am Strong

Though Dark May Seem So Long

For Day Must Follow Every Night

Everything Is Alright

I Am Always Safe From Harm

The Goddess Holds Me In Her Arms

Crystal Magick Spell - Healing

To perform this spell, you will need a black protection crystal of choice, and a piece of rose quartz and the power of your intention.

Hold the crystal in the palm of each hand - and say in thought or out loud:

Wrap Thee In cotton

Bind Thee With Love

Protection From Pain

Surrounds Like A Glove

Brightest Of Blessings

Surrounding Thee This Night

For Though Art Cared For

Healing Thoughts Sent In Flight

Crystal Magick Spell - Love

To perform this spell, you will need a red candle, a crystal of choice and the power of your intention.

Light the candle, and hold the crystal, say in thought or out loud:

I Call Upon Forces Higher Than I

To Awaken The Dreams I Hold Inside

Through This Connection That Knows My Need

I Ask For Love's Enchantment With All Speed

May This Work For Me In The Most Correct Way Attracting

The Love I Need today...

I Call On Thee In Perfect Love & Trust Working

With Me Sending What's Just...

Harming None & Helping All Is How It

Shall Be

This I Make True

By The Law Of 3 Times 3 Times 3

These are just a few you can try. Again, have some fun making your own and creating a spell to suit your personal needs.

A crystal reflects the light that shines into it. If you shine light upon the world, that light will shine back upon you - Lee Horbachewski

BASIC MAGICK

Well my friend we are nearing the end of this journey together. I hope you have enjoyed and felt inspired by some of the learning's within this book. Magick is such a broad subject with so many layers and levels to explore and understand. Like you - I am still learning my craft, - I will always be learning and expanding my knowledge of witchcraft and the power of real magick.

I have shared with you, a lot of the ways I work with magick. Some styles you might love, and some you may not and that is ok. Magick is a personal journey, of self-discovery, a true gift from the universal energy of life -There is no right or wrong way, - as long as you work with purity and true intention in your heart, you cannot go wrong-

<u>WITCH</u>

W - For Wisdom

I - For Integrity

T - For Trust

C - For Compassion

H - For Honour

Values every true Witch abides by - (Lulu Belle)

INDEX OF SPELLS

Abundance Spell – Cinnamon Money Spell	64
Abundance Spell – Friday the 13th	62
Abundance Spell – Prosperity	64
Abundance Spell – To Obtain Money	63
Banishment Spell – Bind a Troublemaker	58
Banishment Spell – Freezer Spell	57
Banishment Spell – Hand Held Mirror	58
Banishment Spell – Remove a Toxic Person or Situation	59
Blessings Magick Spell – New Job Blessings	90
Blessings Magick Spell – Child Blessings	89
Blessings Magick Spell – Home Blessings	88
Blessings Magick Spell – The Gift of Life	87
Blessings Magick Spell – Witches Blessings	88
Candle Magick Spell – Call to Action	124
Candle Magick Spell – Home Protection	125
Candle Magick Spell – Radiant Health	123
Candle Magick Spell – To Find New Employment	125
Candle Magick Spell – Witches Good Luck	123
Crystal Magick Spell – Calming Spell	140
Crystal Magick Spell – Healing	140
Crystal Magick Spell – Love	141
Fertility Magick Spell – Enchanted Egg	102
Fertility Magick Spell – New Life	104
Fertility Magick Spell – Partnership Spell	102
Fertility Magick Spell – Pregnancy	103
Forgetful Magick Spell – Find a Lost Object	83
Forgetful Magick Spell – Forget a Memory	85
Forgetful Magick Spell – Locate A Lost Object	84
Forgetful Magick Spell – Return a Lost Item	83
Forgetful Magick Spell – Return Spell	84
Fruitful Magick Spell – Apple Blessings	108

Fruitful Magick Spell – Orange Upliftment	106
Fruitful Magick Spell – The Bombshell Potion	107
Knot Spell – Basic Love Spell	69
Knot Spell – Knot Your Troubles	68
Knot Spell – Manifestation	67
Love Magick Spell – Clarity	94
Love Magick Spell – Manifest True Love	95
Love Magick Spell – Perfume Spell Attract the Love of Your Life	96
Love Magick Spell – Self-Love for True Love	97
Love Magick Spell – Soul Mate	97
Love Magick Spell – To Bring True Love	96
Moon Magick Spell - Dark Moon Ritual	36
Moon Magick Spell - Full Moon Ritual	34
Moon Magick Spell - Full Moon Wish	34
Moon Magick Spell - New Moon	32
Moon Magick Spell - New Moon Broom Ritual	33
Moon Magick Spell - Waning Moon	35
Moon Magick Spell - Waning Moon Ritual	35
Morning Spell	23
Protection Spell – Banish Bad Luck	45
Protection Spell – Black Candle	45
Protection Spell – Blessings Spell for Cats	50
Protection Spell – Blessing Spell for Dogs	50
Protection Spell – Curse or Hex Reversal	49
Protection Spell – Egg Shell Magick	47
Protection Spell – For Your Family and Loved Ones	47
Protection Spell – Release Negative Energy	45
Protection Spell – To Break a Hex	48
Protection Spell – White Light	45
Self-Healing Spell – Anxiety and Fear	74
Self-Healing Spell – Be at Peace With Self	72

Self-Healing Spell – Confidence 73
Self-Healing Spell – Confidence Ritual 74
Self-Healing Spell – Healing 77
Self-Healing Spell – Release Anger 75
Self-Healing Spell – Self-Esteem Boost 72
Self-Healing Spell – To Banish Depression 75
Self-Healing Spell – To Deal with Grief 76
Self-Healing Spell – To Stop Judgement 77

Friends Of The Witch

Throughout this book I have touched on various ingredients and tools you may feel drawn to getting. I would like to share with you some helpful links. These are all witchy friends of mine. Living their truth and trying to make the world a more gentle place to be in. I am a big believer in supporting and helping small independent business... Should you feel drawn to purchasing any tools for your own witchcraft & magick, please check out these beautiful souls...

Little Treats Of Trean - Crystals...
www.etsy.com/uk/shop/LittleTreatsOfTean
www.facebook.com/TreatsOfTean/

Enchanted Pumpkin - Crystals, Incense, & More...
www.enchantedpumpkin.co.uk
www.facebook.com/enchantedpumpkinunleashthemagic/

The Witch & The Sage - Cauldrons, Herbs, Witchy Tools & More...
www.TheWitchAndTheSage.com
www.facebook.com/The-Witch-The-Sage-148581862395360/

The Witches Coven - Cauldrons, Spell Candles, Wands, Broomsticks & More...
www.etsy.com/uk/shop/TheWitchesCovenJewel
www.facebook.com/thewitchescoven.co.uk/

Fragrantly Magickal - Cauldrons, Spell Candles, Crystals & More...

www.fragrantlymagickal.com
www.facebook.com/FragrantlyMagickal/

Amy's Apothecary - Witchy Home Wares, Natural Skin Care & More...
www.facebook.com/amysapothecaryGB/

Beth James - Astrologer, Holistic Practitioner, Reiki Master...
www.facebook.com/onenesstherapy/

*Magick is a gift not all can see, But for those that can…
Blessed are we - Lady Abigail*

Goodbye Blessings...

May Your Joys Be As Deep As The Oceans

Your Troubles As Light As Its Foam

And May You Find

Sweet Peace Of Mind

Wherever You May Roam

Until we meet again my friend. Blessed Be x

Whatever happens, around the cauldron, stays around the cauldron.

Printed in Great Britain
by Amazon